WATER AND LANDSCAPE

An aesthetic overview of the role of water in the landscape

WATER INFORMATION CENTER, INC.

PERIODICALS

Water Newsletter
Research and Development News
Ground Water Newsletter

BOOKS

Geraghty, Miller, van der Leeden and Troise *Water Atlas of the United States*
Todd *The Water Encyclopedia*
van der Leeden *Ground Water — A Selected Bibliography*
Giefer and Todd *Water Publications of State Agencies*
Soil Conservation Service *Drainage of Agricultural Land*
Gray *Handbook on the Principles of Hydrology*
National Water Commission *Water Policies for the Future*
National Oceanic and Atmospheric Administration *Climates of the States*
Litton, Tetlow, Sorensen and Beatty *Water and Landscape*

The Water Research Association *Groundwater Pollution in Europe*
Meta Systems, Inc. *Systems Analysis in Water Resources Planning*
Giefer *Sources of Information in Water Resources*
van der Leeden *Water Resources of the World*
Todd and McNulty *Polluted Groundwater*

WATER AND LANDSCAPE

An aesthetic overview of the role of water in the landscape

R. BURTON LITTON, JR., Professor
ROBERT J. TETLOW, Associate Professor
   Principal Investigators

JENS SORENSEN, Research Assistant
   Associate Investigator

RUSSELL A. BEATTY, Assistant Professor
   Consultant

Department of Landscape Architecture
University of California
Berkeley, California

Published by
WATER INFORMATION CENTER, INC.
Port Washington, New York

This book is a photographic reproduction of an original, typed manuscript entitled *An Aesthetic Overview of the Role of Water in the Landscape* which was submitted in July, 1971 as a report, under contract, to the National Water Commission to provide background for the Commission's deliberations on the subject of national water policy.

This printing has been undertaken to make this excellent report available in a conventional format for general and reference use.

Published 1974 by Water Information Center, Inc., 14 Vanderventer Ave., Port Washington, N.Y. 11050

Library of Congress Catalog Card Number: 74-79147
ISBN: 0-912394-10-2

Printed in the United States of America

Cover by Nancy Greenberg of Photo Graphics

Preface

Water, through sight and sound, offers distinction to our
surroundings. Whether the environment is being used for work, for
play or habitation there is an enrichment of place by its presence.
This has been true in history and it remains true. Yet how water in
the landscape contributes aesthetic value or adds to environmental
quality is difficult to conceptualize. Because water in its aesthetic
expression is complex - and we are hard pressed to understand our many
responses to it - the tendency is to avoid direct, forthright treatment of the subject and generalities about the goodness of water give
no assistance in recognizing specific enhancement of scenery by water.
Therefore a study of waters' aesthetic role in the landscape is essential.

Since the goal here is to support better planning and improvement
of policy for water's place in the environment, we propose a visual
classification system for fresh water streams and bodies. A set of
descriptive categories are developed in which the three basic elements
of landscape - water, landform, and vegetation - are seen as strongly
interrelated. This initial and concrete step for evaluating water in
its surroundings is taken to address aesthetic quality through the means
of visual components and relationships. We believe such an approach
to aesthetics offers practical assistance to evaluation and planning
for water that is not possible if the subject is treated in a more
abstract way.

But the classifications that can be applied to water in the landscape are not complete or wholly useful without considering the scope
of man-made modifications that may apply. We need to think also in

terms of human use and the provision of facilities concerned with water. It is, then, another goal of this study to suggest how appropriate design and development of man-made elements may be judged for aesthetic merit in the linkage with water.

ACKNOWLEDGMENT

For a study such as this with several investigators and authors, it is desirable to say how responsibilities were shared. As principal investigator, I was concerned with overall structure and direction but the framework eventually evolved as a joint effort -- some of it painfully. More specifically, Sections I and II (photography included) were my prime job. My colleague, Robert Tetlow was also principal investigator, helping with overall organization and was specifically the author of Section III; the drawings for that section are his. Jens Sorensen was research assistant and associate investigator, doing the literature search which gave documentation sources and basic support. The quality comparisons in Section II were made by him, and he set up a majority of the recommendations in Section TV. He gave coordinative assistance and was an indispensable anchor for the whole study. Russell Beatty was consultant on the place of plants and vegetative patterns related to the landscape.

Bruce Sharkey was research assistant during summer 1970. George McKechnie, doctoral candidate in psychology, was of assistance in defining psychological and behavioral aspects of aesthetic experience and research needs. James Pepper, graduate student in landscape architecture, was helpful in providing the perspective in computer application and its research potentials. Ron Williams, also a graduate student in landscape architecture, made the drawings for Section II (figure 7 excepted). Nancy Wakeman and Ava Lydecker were superb in their amiable competance in typing the preliminary drafts and final manuscript. Dr. Tom Scott of the National Water Commission was at all times gracious and helpful to us in attending to the details and interpretation of the contract.

I appreciate the patience, support, and pleasures foregone on the part of our respective families -- research efforts could not be expected to succeed without that.

R. Burton Litton, Jr.
University of California, Berkeley
July 31, 1971

Table of Contents

LIST OF FIGURES

ABSTRACT

Emphasizing the aesthetic aspects of water in the landscape,
this report explores the contributions of water to the environments
of recreation and everyday life. To identify the values of water
in this role, a classification framework is developed for native
characteristics and man-made changes to be considered together. The
scope of the study includes evaluation based on quality recognition
and makes recommendations for needed policies, planning guidelines
and research.

The Introduction (Section I) discusses the constraints of the
study, dependence having been made upon literature search coupled
with the design synthesis of landscape architecture. Interlocked
components making up aesthetic experience are treated briefly, but
the water landscape as environmental stimulus and as a concrete
visual resource is stressed. Concentrating upon the scenic resource
is used as an appropriate limitation for detecting quality - or its
absence - in both natural landscapes and the range of relationships
found in man-made changes.

The Description and Classification Framework (Section II) intro-
duces basic aesthetic criteria - unity, variety, and vividness - which
throughout the study become the generic means of identifying aesthetic
quality. Description and classification can thus be discriminatory.

At the heart of the classification and the study is the development of three different kinds of UNITS. They are the Landscape Unit,

Setting Unit, and the Waterscape Unit. The Landscape Unit is broad
and regional in nature - its importance is integrative. The Setting
Unit is critical for its tangibility, showing water and landscape in
visual combinations - its importance is its reality, establishing the
scene for direct appraisal and management situations. The Waterscape
Unit carries the detailed sense of water and its immediate shore. Together, the three units support a concept of unity, provide different
levels of detail concern and are logical devices for making inventories
and evaluative comparisons. This section ends with a resume on field
inventories (with examples) and applies aesthetic quality comparisons
to selected cases within each of the three different units.

The Classification of Man-made Elements and Improvements (Section
III) emphasizes the fundamental need to recognize Unit characteristics
so that constructed improvements can be made to fit properly. Man-made
structures or alterations are described in five different categories
of elements: linear, area, mass, enclosing, and point. Color and
texture relationships are also discussed. Linear, area and mass
elements are of special importance within the Landscape Unit while
linear, point, and enclosing characteristics, along with color and
texture are more significant in the other two units. Five Evaluative
Terms are described: unifying (importance of total scene), focal
(conscious direction of attention), enclosing (arrangement of positive
enclosure), organizing (formation of coherent pattern, form etc.),
and modifying/enhancing (positive rapport between structures and
landscape). Using these elements and evaluative terms, a quality

comparison of structures and alterations is made within the bounds of the three kinds of Units.

Drawings and photographs are used extensively in Sections II and III for graphic portrayal of principles and to better show elusive concepts.

Recommendations (Section IV) sum up the needs for intra-agency adoption of policies on aesthetic evaluations of water, and suggest planning guidelines to better incorporate aesthetic principles. Various areas of much needed research are outlined. In order to give helpful support to the National Environmental Policy Act, it is urged that there be general adoption among federal agencies of one policy of defining and evaluating water oriented landscapes in which aesthetic criteria are primary tools.

As long as the scenic role of water in the landscape is considered as but a highly personal mental image, little can now be done to have it influence water resource planning and management. The classification framework and its extensions presented here provide a tangible approach to a confusing problem. Environmental enhancement provided by water can be protected, maintained, or developed through application of the principles set forth.

SECTION I

INTRODUCTION

This is about the aesthetic role of water in the landscape.

The environment that surrounds us affects us for better or for

worse. Water as a part of our surroundings has a capacity to fulfill

some human needs for aesthetic appreciation. Whether in the city or

in the wilderness, this seems to be so. Yet we have neglected this

aspect of water as much as we have cherished it.

It is difficult to conceptualize what place water plays, as a

scenic factor, and this study seeks definitions of its aesthetic

contributions to the landscape. There are two basic study objectives:

the first is to develop a visual classification system for fresh

water streams and bodies, proposing descriptive categories showing

interrelationships among water, landforms, and vegetation; the second

is to consider how human use, man-made facilities and manipulations

concerned with water can be called enhancing, compatible, or degrading

to the landscape. Since the nature of the subject is elusive and

requires visualization, heavy dependance is put upon the use of

drawings and photographs.

The 1962 ORRCC report, Water for Recreation: Values and

Opportunities, (U.S.G.S., 1962), makes a strong case for the need

to describe aesthetic and non-monetary aspects of recreation and

it deplores the procedure whereby recreational worth is related to
mass use and that the quality of recreation is given no weight at all.[*]
It notes that there is a great opportunity for leadership on the part
of those who might respond to aesthetic and quality aspects of recreation
and that planning would reflect these concerns. It is abundantly clear
that this kind of leadership has not emerged and we have progressed but
little in the last ten years toward these goals.

We broaden the inference that not only the recreational environment,
but, even more importantly, that of everyday life can be enriched through
sensitive relationships made with water. We see this as another goal
and as an area needing enlightened leadership and planning. This study
is dedicated to those objectives.

This study has been limited by making use of existing literature
and reports which bear upon the role of water in the landscape. While
bibliographic coverage is primarily limited to those materials that
have some direct bearing on our subject, we find support of our thesis
to be fragmentary. From bibliographic material and making use of the
discipline of design - and the field of landscape architecture specifically -
as a means of synthesis, we present this study as a hypothetical framework.

In setting the limitation that water be treated for the aesthetic
role that it plays, a further restriction is that of what may be seen.

---

[*] "In the case of a wild river, one user day might justifiably be
worth 100 or even 1000 user days in an urban picnic area." Wild &
Scenic Rivers Symposium, Herbst and Michaelson (Eds.), 1970.

Water treated in isolation has some of the abstract quality that can
be said to exist in aesthetics. Since it is not the wish to treat
either aesthetics or water in the abstract sense, we will treat water
and the landscape as a linked visual resource. The landscape resource --
or the scenic resource -- is a composition made up of five elements.
These are: the earth, the water, the plants, the animals, and the sky.
We will concentrate upon land elements, water, and plants. Sky and
animals, important as they are, have temporal and ephemeral qualities
which make them exceedingly difficult to treat as compared to the rather
more concrete factors we have chosen. While each of these has expression
in a bewildering set of variations and combinations, this is our framework and a way of restricting our concerns. This also relates to the
fact that planning and management decisions lead to physical changes that
will eventually be seen in the landscape. We seek visual realization of
what those changes will be before they occur.

Taking what is seen as the basic restriction does not deny the
importance of sound, of smell and taste, or of feeling. These other
sensed qualities, particularly as they may be thought of in relation to
water, all together round out the whole. No denial is made, for example,
that sound supports the most powerful expression of water that may at
times be found.* The subtlety of smell may have strength to create a
lasting impression as well. And the cowboy's ballad about cool water

---

* "Only during the few hours of deep sleep, consequent on hard labor,
  has the roar of the waters been hushed." John Wesley Powell, The
  Exploration of the Colorado River, p. 132, Anchor Books, Garden
  City, New York, Doubleday & Co., Inc., 1961.

suggests the importance of feeling, at the same time suggesting a symbol of solace in inhospitable surroundings. Blue water suggests coolness; white water suggests roaring power and sound. Not a small part of the descriptive literature about water has personified it, identifying the ways in which it is felt, heard and smelled.[**] The visual structure of the landscape cannot be stripped of these other secondary characteristics and so they are carried by implication.

It may be useful to say what this study is not. It is not non-visual except as that may be carried through the visual image. It is not a scientific study. There is no concern for trying to measure those qualities and characteristics which are better measured by scientific means. This does not mean, of course, that certain of the elements that are chosen for emphasis may not also have scientific implications about them. Scientific suggestion can add to aesthetic richness. This study will not carry an emphasis of behavioral response to the landscape and to water for the very simple reason that there is so little information in this area. We will not make conjectures about what the landscape and associated water means to the beholder. As references are found in literature and in studies by others which do deal with meaning or response, those findings will be cited.

Empirical data confirming or refuting aesthetic attributes of the landscape and of water are essentially non-existant. This kind of environmental assessment represents a new field with substantial work

---

[**] Mark Twain, Life on the Mississippi; Sidney Lanier, "Song of the Chattahoochee"; H.D. Thoreau, "On the Concord and Merrimac", "The Allegash and the East Branch".

yet to be accomplished (Craik, 1970). Indeed, for some it may be a
contradiction in terms to say that the nature of aesthetic investigation
be scientifically posed. At this stage, then, it is our objective to
set forth hypotheses and to be orderly in our expressions which will be
dependent upon the vehicle of the visual landscape.

General Components of Aesthetic Experience

A brief discussion of the general components of aesthetic experience
under consideration here is the often complex response of the observer-
user to a particular landscape. Three general variables define this
relationship: the observer's "state of mind" e.g., such as his current
perceptual set, past experiences, future expectations, and environmental
life style (Meier, 1969); the context of observation (e.g. boating,
photographing, swimming), and the environmental stimulus itself.[1]

[1]
Craik (1970) has presented a somewhat more elaborate "Paradigm for
Research on the Comprehension of Environmental Displays," consisting of
four components: Observer, Media of Presentation, Response format,
and Environmental Dimensions. Here our context of observation
combines Craik's Media of Presentation and Response Format while
the classes are respectively equivalent.

Observer's State of Mind

It is clear that observers differ in the aesthetic qualities
they attribute to a landscape. This may be a function largely of
the anticipated recreational use for the area. The person who
approaches an area with the intention of sightseeing will undoubtedly
have a different aesthetic experience than the person who is
oriented toward more active water pursuits such as fishing, boating
or swimming. The particular anticipated activity will to some
degree determine the psychological set (expectations and desires)
which the observer brings to the situation and thus his experience
of it. Is the observer passing by on his way to work and thus
having only incidental contact with a particular water area, or
will he vacation there? These are role or behavioral determinants
of the observer's state of mind.

Is the motivation that of desire for social interaction? Is
the landscape approached as a place conducive to social gathering,
(Gray, 1970) to meet friends or to seek companions, or is the
observer-user more interested in getting away from people (Hendee,
et al, 1968). What attitudes does he have toward the environment?
Does he approach the environment with a particular cultural belief
system (Kluckhohn and Strodtbeck, 1903)? Is his appreciation of
water resources a function of having grown up in a drought plain

(Saarinen, 1966) or in a city (Paar, 1967). These are differences
in environmental dispositions (McKechnie, 1970).

What ethnic background has he grown up in? Are there sex
role determinants of aesthetic response? Are there age or life
cycle stage differences (Hendee, et al., 1968). Are highly educated people
more appreciative of undeveloped water resources? (Wildavsky, 1967)?
These are demographic determinants of aesthetic responsiveness.

Context of Observation

Apart from the observer's state of mind are the matters of
1) the events which occur as one approaches a place or an environment and 2) the things which actually take place upon arrival. The
mode of travel (air, foot, auto, bicycle, boat, train, bus), con-
commitant rate of movement from one place to another certainly are
important considerations when analyzing aesthetic response. Did
the observer arrive by air, leaving one environment, passing over
many people and other environments and arrive at his destination
in quick order - creating generalized but perhaps dilute impressions
of what transpired enroute? Or did he backpack a few long miles
with spartan effort and quiet self-satisfaction? The motorist, the
boater, the pedestrian - each with his particular means of movement and rate of advance - can expect to gather different impressions
with different levels of detail and to attribute different qualities
to the surroundings encountered enroute.

The context of observation is also determined in part by the
sequence of events or experiences that accrue from travel (Clawson

and Knetsch, 1966). Was access easy or was it difficult? Did it take a long time or was it a short period? Was it a long time or was it a short period? Was it a long way or was it a short one? During the course of travel were there bland landscapes or bland experiences along the way or were they exhilarating? Was there a sequential build-up from things less interesting to things more interesting? Or did the sequence of events go so that apparently more interesting things were encountered first and being left behind, there was a let-down arrival? Sequences of events marking the passage of time spent in route represents the way we normally see a landscape (or for that matter a building). Residues of past memories are combined with the experiences of the present and anticipations of the future, yielding a complex temporal texture.

Is the observer high above or low down with respect to what he is able to see (Litton and Craik, 1970). Can he move about, and choose whether he is high above, intermediately above, or close to the landscape? Is the viewing opportunity complicated by screening? What is the way - terrain or vegetation? Are there other obstructions or deterrents? Are observation opportunities lessened because of surroundings which are degraded or otherwise unsatisfactory?

Actions taken at the time of arriving or being at a place presumably also have an influence. If it is a short term stay, perhaps the action is instant recreation, an immediate launching of the boat, a quick grab for the camera. Perhaps the intent is to stay longer and so the first thing is to establish accommodations, to unpack, to change clothes, to get ready for specific action or to do what needs to be done. Then, is it a matter of plunging in, finding out for oneself or is it asking the management what is to be done next?

The observer's state of mind and the context of observation then pose a galaxy of conditions that suggest the complexity of the problem of defining what an aesthetic experience may consist of.

The Environmental Stimulus

A full analysis of the aesthetic experience requires an objective appraisal of the stimulus array itself. Such analysis might typically involve a valid and intersubjectively reliable description of geographic, geological, and /or design attributes of the stimulus. The choice of actual rating dimensions in any case is crucial, because it defines apriori the universe within which the description must take place.

For our purposes, it is useful to subdivide environmental stimuli into two classes; those aspects which are visual and those which are non-visual (i.e., those which are sensed by non-visual means, for example noise or odors.) Our study concentrates particularly on the visual attributes of the physical environment.

For example, should the environment be described in terms of model adjectival descriptors of everyday language, or should more formal rating systems be utilized (e.g. Litton and Craik's topology of landscape scenes, Appleyard's analytic attribute system or Theil's sequential notational system)? Should the physical, behavioral, or geographic attributes of the environment be measured? Empirical research on these issues will undoubtedly show that different classifications of environmental stimuli (e.g., physical versus geographic) will have differing explanatory value for various observers under differing contexts of observation.

A Model of Aesthetic Response

The following model is intended to represent aesthetic response and show schematic interrelationships. It is a conceptually simple model, and does not attempt to capture the psychological subtlety of, for example, Peterson or Neuman's (1969) conceptual model of individual preference process. Here environmental stimuli (mostly visual for our purposes) impinge on the observer, who processes or interprets them in terms of his own past experiences, beliefs, and current emotional states, (his "state of mind") and also in terms of the context of observation (e.g., position, movement, time of year). These latter factors do, in fact, determine to some extent which stimuli will be a part of the observer's contiguous visual environment. The perception and processing of environmental stimuli by the observer within the context of observation results in an aesthetic experience. Notice that the various components of the observer's "state of mind" and the context of observation may be ordered in such a manner as to yield a continuum ranging from those which are mostly a function of the observer independent of the context of observation (e.g. physiological conditions or emotional states), to those which are context bound and essentially observer-free (e.g. position-viewability, distance, etc.). This suggests, of course, that the observer-context distinction is in some sense arbitrary and that the specification of the context necessarily requires an observer-- objective though he might be.

12

Figure A

A Model of Aesthetic Response

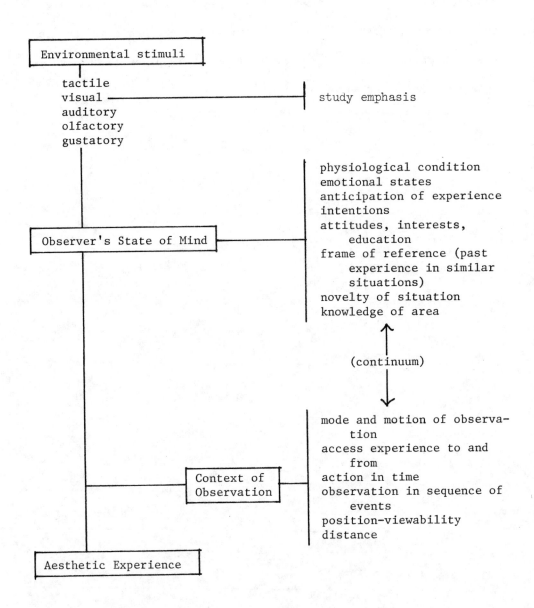

Perspective on the Visual Resource

Environmental stimuli defined in this study are the visual components and relationships found in water, terrain, and plants. These can be put in perspective with the other two factors - the observer's state of mind and the context of his observation. While for some the landscape is more a state of mind than it is a set of physical parameters (Nash, 1967, Lowenthal, 1967) yet the assumption made here is that a state of mind depends upon a reaction from environmental stimuli. To reaffirm the objectives and limitations of this study, the visual landscape is used as a display of tangible evidence within which we can find the presence or absence -- or some measure -- of aesthetic quality. Considering the landscape as a visual display also poses the matter of manipulations and man-made changes which may be seen as compatible or incompatible with the display. It is only appropriate that this design overview study deals with tangible, visible, physical elements and relationships in the outdoors.

SECTION II

DESCRIPTION AND CLASSIFICATION FRAMEWORK

This section consists of three parts; the classification, the inventory, and the evaluation. While these parts are separated for purposes of convenient discussion, they should be thought of together and attendant upon one another. While each represents a special step or procedure, their coordination and simplification depends upon the identification of conspicuous, vivid combinations of elements within which quality may be recognized. To set a tone and a constraint for discussions to follow, an understanding of basic aesthetic criteria can direct effort toward the identification of quality. This avoids entanglement with the impossible and fruitless task of trying to identify all of the characteristics and qualities that may be found in the landscape.

To avoid burial by details, we subscribe to this advice:

"It is far more important that a scheme of classification recognize the existence of... different aspects of water than be excessively concerned with the details of the classification categories." (USGS 1962; ORRRC, 1962). It is imperative, then, to attend to those things which can be distinguished and to set aside those things which cannot be.

Basic Aesthetic Criteria

The three basic aesthetic criteria are _unity_, _variety_, and _vividness_. While these are abstract, they will be interpreted in more direct and realistic terms in the text.

Unity:[*]

Water by its very nature of being different from land, and in that
sense contrasting to land, is seen as continuous and as a whole. This
is true for linear stream or spreading lake. The stream in its natural
state starts as a small trickle which maintains its continuity while
growing and changing up to its meeting with the sea. Whether the one-
ness of moving continuity, the wholeness of surface, or the singleness of
one material, the expression still lies with its unity. Even beyond that
long continuity represented by the stream from beginning to end or the
lake with its continuous, level surface, there is also the recognition of
unity in subparts or sections. Unity is not simple. There is the ecological unity of stream course and shore (Craighead and Craighead, 1962).
There is hydrological river system unity(Leopold, 1962). There is
aesthetic or design unity – the unification of water as a material and
surface (Hubbard and Kimball, 1917). To the degree that any of these
kinds of unity may be recognized, they can be taken to represent forms
of aesthetic quality.

Variety:

Variety is potentially the enemy of unity, but it is one quality from
which strength and interest in evolved.[**] Leopold (1962) comments that general

---

* "It is neither the presence or the absence of this or that part, or
shape, or color that wins our eye in natural objects. It is the consistency and harmony of the parts juxtaposed, the subordination of
details to masses to the whole." Horatio Greenough, Form and Function, 1947.p.

** "So various are the characters which water can assume that there is
scarcely an idea in which it may not occur or an impression which it
cannot enforce." (Moore, 1957).

river characteristics include a pervasive unity despite their having
tremendous diversity, these two things together being the most important
characteristic of river systems. That variety may be expressed through
movement, through color, through differences of edge. The response of
water to weather and atmospheric conditions, to light and to depth and
bottom have been equated to personalities and living characteristics.
Quick to respond or slow, this somewhat mysterious, seemingly unpredictable
behavior of water, seems to say something of its intrique to the human
observer (Morisawa and Murie, 1969).[*] To the degree that the greatest
amount of richness or diversity may be seen, the inference is then also
the greater the aesthetic quality. Obviously, that variety or richness
depends not only upon water, but upon land elements and plants associated
with it and their synthesis into a composition.

Vividness:

Vivid combinations of water with land and with plants can as readily
be satisfactory as unsatisfactory, good or bad. Yet, recognition of
quality is the intent here. Contrast is an obvious way of saying that
something is vivid. It may be the presence of fast water immediately
against slow water (Dearinger, 1968), of water in powerful opposition to
gorge constriction, or the reflection of tree images upon the surface of
dark pools. The contrast of conspicuous combinations may be those which
depend upon interesting landscape-water linkages as well as upon time
and sequence (U.S. Army Corps - USDA-USDI, 1969). The still water
stream that suddenly changes to swift and fast water may be understood

---

[*] "If there is magic on this planet - it is contained in water." Loren
Eisley, 1959, The Immense Journey, p. 15.

only over time or by repeated exposure. What may be called an ordinary
stream may have its moments and its segments which are anything but
ordinary. "The streams themselves have a very interesting character –
they may be placid and calm in dry seasons but fierce and forbidding in
times of heavy rainfall." Ibid.

While this preliminary discussion of ways for recognizing quality
is necessarily dilute and overly simplified, it serves as an introduction
to the point of view we assume. A more elaborate presentation of these
aesthetic criteria will be found in Section II – Evaluation.

CLASSIFICATION

A classification for water in the landscape based upon visual characteristics is considered essential so that inherent native conditions are recognized, evaluated, and used with sensitivity. A systematic procedure for comprehensive evaluation of water-landscape quality can provide a means of communication and more general understanding. Establishment of certain elements and criteria making up a classification framework (as agreed upon) should lead toward objectivity of appraisal and away from narrow subjectivity.

Setting up a classification procedure is approached with considerable trepidation. Caution is based upon the fact that classification is artificial and in the varied continuum that water represents in the landscape, there are no neat and precise category boxes. Yet, we propose classification units which are admitted to be arbitrary in that there will be a transition among them. A quotation seems appropriate as we start: "Nature abhors classification. In using the concept of the stream erosion cycle -- the boundaries between stages are indistinct, few rivers approach the ideal condition, and many rivers may show all the stages, but not necessarily in the expected order, several times between their sources and their mouths." (Scovel, et al, 1965, p. 87)

In the establishment of a classification procedure concerning water in the landscape, we believe a regional constraint to be critically important in maintaining localized quality of native

environment. Characteristics and visual quality of such areas as

the Wyoming Basin, the Arkansas Valley, or the Catskills -- each

a section of different physical provinces -- are clearly different.

Yet one cannot be the substitute for another even if the quality of

one were to be determined as higher than for another. Each has

importance in its own locality even if it may command but little

use or recognition beyond its locality (Cain, 1968).

The Concept of Unity and Visual Units

Unity as a visual quality of water in the landscape has been

pointed out in the introduction. The concept of unity is stressed

as primary to the objective of recognizing and maintaining aesthetic

quality. Visual units are proposed as tools in serving that object-

ive, being used for classification, inventory, evaluation, and planning

and design development.

The classification framework is built upon the delineation of

three different units. These are the Landscape Unit, the Setting

Unit, and the Waterscape Unit. Choice of the word "unit" is meant

to suggest the tangible evidence of a visually conspicuous entity.

A unit is limited; it can be singled out and identified. Combination

of the three different units can be integrated to cover visual stream

and lake systems to support the concept of unity.

Landscape, setting, and waterscape units vary respectively in

character from the more general to the very specific. The three

units identified represent scale differences from very large to
relatively small, but there must be room for inconsistencies of
size or scale variations. While it would be convenient to say that
the landscape unit as the largest would be expected to contain a
number of setting units and, in turn, the setting units would contain a number of waterscape units, this might not be so. This
scale relationship might occur, yet the classification needs to be
flexible enough to recognize variations in the landscape that will
not fit a set regime.

The setting unit is emphasized as perhaps most important of the
three units because of tangible relationships between water and landscape - managerially and in design manipulation it is critical. It
is distinguished as the landscape which is the surrounding container
for any body of water, the two together establishing the setting.
Sometimes the landscape may be dominant; sometimes the water may
be dominant. The landscape unit is important in a contextual or
integrative way. A landscape unit is usually made up of a series of
similar or visually related setting units. In this way it achieves
a cohesion in the regional sense. Its quality will be eroded if
apparently small and isolated manipulations in water-landscapes
(setting or waterscape units) are made with failure to consider their
broader regional implications. The waterscape unit carries the
detail sense of water _per se_ and serves as the vehicle within which
that specific element is carefully considered. It is made up of

water and shore elements. The three units are mutually dependent,
each affects the other in terms of character, quality, or manipulations.

Units may be clear and sharp with hard boundaries within which
consistent character and few distracting complexities exist. They may
also, however have diffused boundaries. They may have internal complexities that are visually confusing. To qualify in terms of quality
the sense of unit should be clear and complete. But units which are
diffuse or which lack clarity do serve the important function of making
connection with more positive units -- they do serve in unification
and as visual foils for more distinguished companion units.

Figure B

Classification Framework:

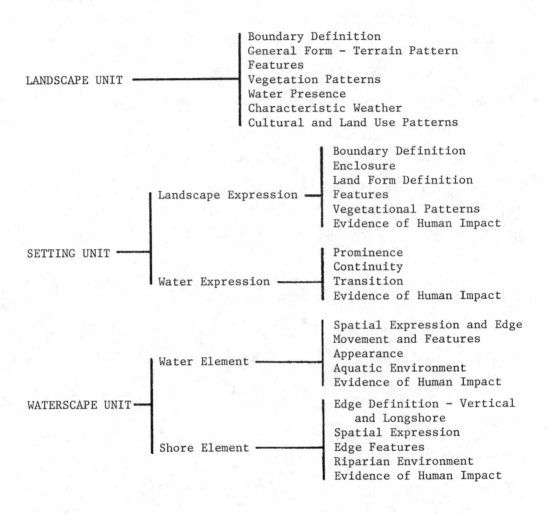

LANDSCAPE UNIT ——————
Boundary Definition
General Form - Terrain Pattern
Features
Vegetation Patterns
Water Presence
Characteristic Weather
Cultural and Land Use Patterns

SETTING UNIT ——————

Landscape Expression ——
Boundary Definition
Enclosure
Land Form Definition
Features
Vegetational Patterns
Evidence of Human Impact

Water Expression ——————
Prominence
Continuity
Transition
Evidence of Human Impact

WATERSCAPE UNIT ——

Water Element ——————
Spatial Expression and Edge
Movement and Features
Appearance
Aquatic Environment
Evidence of Human Impact

Shore Element ——————
Edge Definition - Vertical
    and Longshore
Spatial Expression
Edge Features
Riparian Environment
Evidence of Human Impact

THE LANDSCAPE UNIT

The landscape unit has large scale distinction and suggests a regional or geographic context, such as the section of a physical province or of the "natural landscape series."[*] The natural landscape regions delineated in the State of California (Mason, 1970) represent a similar kind of connotation within which the unit may achieve identity. The California Protected Waterways Plan, 1971, has been tied to these landscape regions. In visual terms, the unit could also be a discreet part of a physiographic section. The scale would be such that visibility of the whole would be possible only over a period of time and through an extended experience (Iowa State U., 1969). Air flights over the area should be considered critically necessary to give definition as would be the collective memory of it. This unit necessarily contains a series of characteristic streams or water bodies as an essential part, providing a special differentiation from setting and waterscape units in which a single stream, a single lake or connected lakes are typical.

Generalized impressions rather than detail characterize the landscape unit. Attendant in obtaining a sense of overview, it is assumed that the observer is high looking into or down upon the unit from a number of set points or from an air flight overview. The sense of generality is supported by the idea of distant or intermediately distant views rather than close up. The observer whose job it is to delineate this large scale unit must put himself in

[*] Definition: "Areas judged to have cohesiveness defined by 'the general visual impression gained from the repetition of a dominant form over a large area.'" (Research Planning and Design Associates, Inc., 1967).

the frame of mind to observe general framework characteristics of the landscape and water with it, rather than to be caught by the more precise demands of detail.

Any large series of related lakes or especially an extended stream could be expected to embrace a number of landscape units. For example, the Sacramento River in California would have landscape units defined in (1) upper reaches or mountain tributary phases, (2) a piedmont or foothill phase describing a transition unit between the upper tributary area and the Central Valley unit, (3) a central section or valley phase, and (4) a lower delta dominated phase. This particular river would, then, be described within no less than four landscape units, contained primarily in two of California's physical provinces and touching upon a third.[*] Somewhat primarily, landscape units for this river could be referenced to California's natural landscape areas (Mason, 1970).

Boundary Definition

Boundary definition consists of the application of certain aspects of the several components which make up the landscape unit. These components consist of general form, terrain pattern, features, dominant vegetative patterns, water presence, characteristic weather and cultural patterns. The definition of edge then, extracts from the whole group of components. Boundary definition consists of determining the edges which are created between dissimilar things or contrasting elements. Sharp edges need to be recognized for

[*] State of California, Department of Natural Resources, Division of Mines, Olaf P. Jenkins, Chief, Geomorphic Map of California, Bulletin 158, 1938.

their capacity to evoke strong visual images, yet some edges or margins will be transition zones or mixed areas between two elements. Adjacent units can join with a confused sense of identity and their junction could include an extensive area. While such mixed zones or margins may be sufficiently big to be actually designated as units, they do not well fit the definition. However such areas serve the important function of continuity between defined units and this characteristic needs to be recognized.

The boundary definition may occur in one of two ways: first, it is visual by reason of native components seen in juxtaposition, such as expressed in ridge and skylines, horizon planes, water margins or vegetative type change edges (Iowa State U., 1969). A second type of visual boundary definition can come out of the contrast between natural or unaltered conditions as opposed to altered conditions (Lewis, 1968; Research Plan and Design Associates, 1968. Alterations could be either man-caused or be the product of natural catastrophe.

Junctions involving general form such as the meeting between mountain range and hill range are apt to be a subtle or inconspicuous joining rather than positive delineation. A junction of maximum impression would be that of mountain range against plain -- for example, vertical against the horizontal such as the east escarpment of the Sierra Nevada against valleys of the Basin Ranges. Terrain patterns are also repetitious expressions of general form. As long as repetition (e.g. rolling hills) is carried on, it will assist in defining a unit. Where that repetition ceases or breaks

26

Fig. 1 - Boundary definition made by junction of
natural and altered landscapes

Fig. 2 - Landscape unit identified by continuity
of native landscape components

down and joins either steeper slopes or more level plain, an edge or
junction is marked.

Some boundaries are those seen between altered and unaltered
conditions. Fire as natural catastrophe can give an area identity,
although dubious in terms of quality. The Tillamook burn (Oregon),
now nearly 40 years old, is still characterized by standing snags and
successional vegetative cover. Lands representing managerially
different conditions such as areas in which timber is harvested are
visually contrasted to land areas in the Wilderness System. The
highly distinctive farm country of Lancaster County, Pennsylvania,
has rolling hills with contour strip crops, blocks of woodlot groves,
a dispersed pattern of farmhouse-barn complexes and small villages all
together present the visual sense of unit. Or the slack water impoundments of man-made lakes, perhaps seasonally marked by conspicuous
drawdown edges constitute a form of identity that may be central to a
landscape unit; the reservoir series along the upper Missouri or the
Tennessee Valley drainage are examples.

Features at the landscape unit scale are more properly collective
features rather than individual. Peaks and pinnacles of the Sawtooth
Range, for example, show a powerful dominance around their surroundings
and they can define a unit by being the central element of a unit. So
also with gorge or a deep ravine system which could be the skeletal
center of a unit rather than a side margin.

Water presence, whether abundant or scarce, could help give unit
definition. A large and obvious pattern of either river system or
lake systems could help determine limits. A chain of cirque lakes in

a mountain basin could well be the heart of a landscape unit, the
Great Salt Lake Basin and attendant streams, or the morainal lakes
of western Minnesota could be also.

Characteristic weather can also help give definition. This is
most apt to be expressed in vegetation changes such as those of the
east side of the Wind River range in semi-desert or the east side of
the Sierra Nevada with rain shadow effect. Both of these are visually
contrasted against the composition of the more well watered western slope.
The zone of summer coastal fog or redwood region of the California-
Oregon Coast Range can also be seen as finite.

General Form - Terrain Pattern

General form relates primarily to the expression of landform,
and there are four different categories. The first, and most easily
distinguished, consists of upright projective or convex forms found
collectively as mountain or hill ranges (See Fig. 2). Mountains by
reason of implied larger scale and more commanding angular line
character are visually contrasted against the softer, curving lines
and smaller scale of hills. The second group would constitute those
which are generally flattened and distinguished as plains or plateaus.
Horizontally placid, their capacity to impress will depend upon sheer
expanse or in being a display foil against which upright forms may be
seen.

Fig. 3 - General form contrast of rising mountain range
with adjacent flat plain, Grand Teton Range

The third category would be that demonstrating or showing concavity,
the recognition of depressed, bowl-like containment, but on a broad and
open scale. Valleys or valley streams and basins are the essence of
this. Basins may be difficult to distinguish, however from the flattened forms of plain or plateau.

The last expression is a composite in which either flattened planes
or concave surfaces are accompanied by isolated peaks, cones, or other
vertical, projecting elements. This would be expressed in the Snake
River plain of Idaho or the Navajo country. Water presence in actual-
ity, in dry washes, or as represented in riparian fingers, will be a

visually important component, especially in the open, horizontal
expressions of general form.

Terrain pattern emerges from general form through repetition
of form-shape-color-texture variations (Iowa State U., 1969). It is
intimately linked with water as an associate, the two together being
agent and product. Starting with the simplicity of a level yet normally directive slope, the sense of a land-water pattern may emerge
less from the mass presence of water than by vegetation that is the
accompaniment of water. As form becomes more discernable in being
rolling, ridged, or a combination of undulating hills and swales,
pattern begins to emerge three dimensionally. As slopes steepen
they may be distinguished either by their maintaining relatively
simple surface faces or they may become highly disected (See Figs. 4
and 5). At the other end of the continuum would be the pattern consisting of mountainous forms in which ascendant and upright thrust
peaks will be major determinants. The sense of pattern will be largely revealed along skylines but also as ridgelines, separated in space
and seen against more distant similar images.

Fig. 4 – Terrain pattern: coarse grain dissection

Fig. 5 – Terrain pattern: fine grain dissection

Features

Features at the scale of the landscape unit are necessarily
large or recognized through their collective structure. Features
lie at the heart of aesthetic quality through the ways in which
they stand out, through dominant scale, through isolation, through
distinctive skyline, or some other special characteristic such as
surface contrast and variation. At this level, features could be
divided into two kinds: those being landform elements and those
which are of water. The peaks and pinnacles of the Teton Range or
of the Sawtooth in Idaho are collective range features which stand
out in their isolation and their contrast to basal lakes and surrounding flats. Segments of both ranges include the enrichment of
water-land contrasts: differences of material, color, movement, the
reflection of secondary images.

Fig. 6 - Range feature reinforced by basal lake,
Grand Teton Range

Limestone cliffs, escarpments and outcrops constitute a system
of features along the Obed and associated rivers in Tennessee. So
also the gorges and canyons of the Little Colorado constitute a continuing feature overshadowing the water below -- but testimony to the
power of water. White water stretches of the main Colorado or the
Horse-Shoe-Niagara Falls constitute large scale water features, becoming dominant to areas beyond themselves. A lake system characteristic of alpine glaciation could constitute a collective feature, as
could those morainal lakes of Wisconsin and Minnesota (See Fig. 10).

Fig. 7 - "Collective feature" at the landscape
unit scale, Sawtooth Range, Idaho

Vegetation Patterns

The character of some landscapes is determined in good measure by
particular kinds or compositions of vegetative cover (Morisawa, Murie,
1969; Dearinger, 1968; Whitman, 1968). At the larger scale of the
landscape unit, this is expressed in patterns of very generalized
vegetation types such as forest, woodland, scrub or chaparral, grassland, and barren areas. Agricultural or man-made types are also included. At this level of concern, individual vegetation types are
seen for their broad gauge characteristics of color, texture, density,

and marginal connection with other cover types or water.

A significant role of vegetation in the landscape unit is the definition of boundaries. Sharp changes in plant types associated with topographic, soil, or climatic changes - with contrasting junctions produced - can indicate a landscape unit boundary. The line where valley grassland or agricultural cropland meets foothill brush or savannah would indicate such a boundary. In all likelihood a particular vegetative cover will be associated with a particular landform system - the visual elements of surface and form reinforcing one another.

A number of visual relationships between vegetative patterns and the presence of water in the landscape unit can be reviewed for their distinctive characteristics. It is assumed that these combinations of water-plant meetings are a repetitive pattern at this scale. On the western slopes of the Cascades, the simple continuity of the dark fir forest moves like a blanket to the fingered edge of the timberline; lakes and streams are tightly embraced except as there may be narrow rims of alder and bigleaf maple about the water edges. In Colorado, the lodge-pole-spruce-fir forest is also a continuous blanket but, for example, a combination of blue spruce and aspen patches will make the linear patterns of stream courses. In the Appalachian landscape, the hardwood forests flow on, giving a screen canopy to the smaller streams and with only larger river and lake surfaces being revealed. Quite an opposite pattern would be found along the San Juan or Pecos River with cottonwood strings flagging the water courses, revealing water presence in summer by light green tree rows seen against the sere gray-brown plateau sage.

Fig. 8 – Continuous forest pattern broken by
water pattern contrast

Fig. 9 – Cottonwood string flagging the water
course, North Platte River, Wyoming

Each of these vegetation patterns asssociated with water can be assessed for differences of quality that come from their store of variety and expression of vividness. But each is also of regional importance that can be attached to their being integral parts of spacific landscape units.

Water Presence

Within the landscape unit large scale or gross characteristics of the presence of water are distinguishing marks. First of all, it may be a question of occurrence -- much water as opposed to little. The presence of large amounts of water does not necessarily make it more distinctive despite its being or becoming a dominant character- istic (Research Planning and Design Associates, 1968; U.S.B.O.R.. May 1970). In the general human experience, the sight of water is relative- ly rare compared with the everyday view of the land surface which surrounds us and that we move upon (Moore, 1957). Small amounts of water in arid countries have the capacity to evoke a strong image through the device of contrast (Research Planning and Design Associates, 1968; Water Resources Engineers, 1970). Beyond the mere presence of water is the importance of characteristic patterns of its dispersion through the landscape. Such diverse expressions as coarse fingered streams or kettle ponds and marshes speak of particular places.

In the overview, the capacity for water to reflect light or to be seen as having a color different from adjacent land will give notice.

Fig. 10 - Lake system overview with dominant
presence of water

For a country characteristically covered by continuous forest

such as the west slope of the Cascades, water may be quite hidden and

be subtly expressed in the larger unit. (See Fig. 8). Identity of

water is then apt to be transferred either to the special classes of

plants which associate with water or otherwise water may be buried

in the defiles of the land pattern. The more open landscapes

associated with older river patterns of meanders are apt to be more

revealing of water than are the straighter courses of water in younger

landscapes where containment within close defiles tends to conceal. Yet,

there is an interesting comparison between older and younger streams. (See

Figs. 11 and 12). The placid and serene passage of water in the mature

stream with greater likelihood of visibility must be compared
against the active, swift and perhaps white flow of water in the
younger stream where terrain tends to screen. For the observer on
the ground, however, the steeper gradients of the younger stream,
including vertical or near vertical water surfaces, does give
viewing advantages. Man-made influence on water can also come out
of the comparison between slack water or impounded water areas as
opposed to those stretches which flow freely.*

---

* "The freer parts of the river complement the larger impoundments."
U.S. BOR, The Middle Missouri, 1968.

Fig. 11 - More active and varied stream associated
with younger landscape

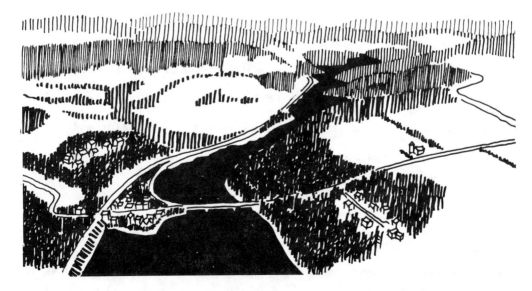

Fig. 12 - More placid and uniform stream associated
with mature landscape

Characteristic Weather

Weather in its seasonal expectations and regional relationships can give definition to the landscape unit in several ways (Morisawa and Murie, 1969). The first is in the weather phenomenon itself shown in such a ways as the summer fog along the west coast of the California coastal range. This can be contrasted to the Sierra Nevada summer climate of clear mornings and afternoon tendency for cloud buildup, perhaps leading to thunderstorms in afternoon or evening. So also in the Appalachain Piedmont where summer weather may be characteristically accompanied by afternoon storms and cloud development. These are visual aspects of climate or weather in a particular place. On the Great Plains the sky with cloud formations constitutes a very major part of the whole landscape scene. Thus, clouds whether high or low, and precipitation whether fog, rain or snow, and their antithesis -- the clear sky; these give visual evidence of places that can be distinguished.

Secondly, there is the direct result of how climate effects visual aspects and changes on the landscape. The hotter, drier climate can give water a different value than that of cooler and wet climates. Each patch of water, in the arid landscape, takes on the distinction of a feature. In wetter landscapes, water -- though dominant -- may seem only monotonous or an impediment to movement. There are also the ways in which vegetation responds to climate and microclimates. The sparse and irregular vegetation complexes of the east side of the Wind River Range or the Sierra Nevada have been mentioned as contrasting to the dense and complete conifer covers of their west side slopes. Coastal and more humid climates tend to encourage continuous forests with but subtle hints of water presence from riparian vegetation. The microclimates of Utah or Idaho hills and mountains are suggested by grass or barren south faces contrasted to conifer covers on the north.

These are but a sample of how climate, landscape, and water may be joined up within the landscape unit.

Cultural and Land Use Patterns

Margins between wildlands and agricultural land can mark the edge of the landscape unit. Or the heart of the unit may be characterized by evidence of human occupation, such as the highly distinctive mosaic of field crops, woodlots, pastures, farmstead centers and sinuous streams in the Pennsylvania Dutch country. Rectangular crop patterns, buttressed by range-township road lines, with meandering streams and small ponds -- many man-made -- are characteristic of the Great Plains. They are made prominent as they butt up against the dissimilar patterns -- native and humanized -- of the east front range of Colorado.

These collective man-influenced characteristics are part of the matrix identified with the landscape unit. Within it the more specialized expressions of water -- freeflowing, impounded, channelized, in ponds or lakes, in distinguishable combinations -- can be evaluated and given special attention.

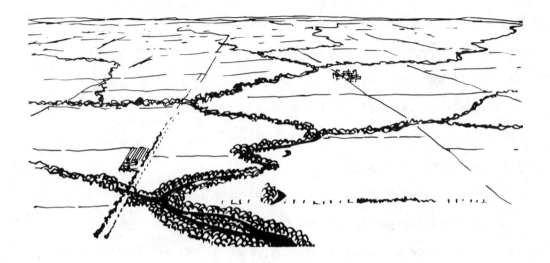

Fig. 13 - Agricultural land use pattern combined
with Great Plains stream system

THE SETTING UNIT

The setting unit is primarily defined as a visual corridor or
envelope of space which is set by enclosure of land forms or forest
edges (Litton, 1968; Lewis, 1964; Wisconsin, 1963). The sense of
enclosure is dependent upon the observer being within the space,
especially in a position closely oriented to any water bodies
present. (USDI and Federal Interdepartment Task Force, 1968).
Visibility of the whole unit will normally be built upon a series of
viewing points, some of which may be relatively high looking down-
ward toward the floor. Yet, occasionally it might be possible
that the definition of the unit could be seen from $360°$ about a
single point.

Water as a stream or lake - or visually linked lakes - is assumed
to be a central element within the unit. Included water elements may
be visually strong or weak. While water is important in generation
of interest, different levels of balance between water and landscape
should be most apparent within this unit. (U.S. National Park Service,
1968). As an important point of differentiation, the presence of a
single water body is implied for the setting unit, while a series of
repeated water bodies is to be expected within the larger scaled,
more generalized landscape unit.

The size, configuration and boundary edges can be expected to
vary within wide limits. While it is conceivable that the setting
unit could rival its related landscape unit in size or expanse, the
usual expectation is that of a series of smaller setting units found

within the matrix of the larger landscape unit. (Research Planning
and Design Associates, 1967; Iowa State U., 1969).

Configuration of the unit may be compared to the idea of "floor
plan" that varies from simple to complex. A lake shape can introduce
the concept of simple or complex unit form. An outline such as a
regular oval is easily grasped and has initial strength due to its
simplicity and visual unity. However, a more complex type with, for
example, a series of side embayments will have more intrigue over
time because of built in variety. (Research Planning and Design
Associates, 1968). Quality of a unit, then, could be derived from
distinction of configuration -- clarity of its overall shape, from
a sense of its wholeness of unification, and from included varied.
(Compare Figs. 14 and 15).

Boundary definition depends very largely upon enclosure edges.
Some units can be expected to have distinct and sharp boundaries --
others will be incomplete or indefinite in their margins. A single
setting unit can also display a combination of very positive to very
fuzzy edges -- such as nearly enclosure compared to that in the
distance. But, quite apart from edge of boundary, the central bottom
of a setting unit with water displayed dominantly can also give
definition and distinction.

In order to clarify the nature of the setting unit and its
quality the discussion following will consider influential factors of
landscape and water character.

Fig. 14 - Simple, circular lake implies
simple unit configuration

Fig. 15 - Complex lake shape implies a more
varied setting unit

Landscape Expression

While most of the elements concerned with landscape expression
are oriented toward the earth oriented elements or landform, water
is so closely knit to earth that no clean separation between the
two can be made. There are five factors which contribute to landscape expression. They consist of 1) boundary definition 2) enclosure,
3) landforms, 4) features, and 5) vegetation patterns. The impacts
of human use can also be expected to be of special significance in
affecting landscape character here. Under the headings of boundary
definitions and features it is convenient to include certain aspects
of water definition.

Boundary Definition

Boundary definition is that tangible concern with the visual
margins or edges of the setting unit. While the basic relationships
among things which enables us to see - outlines, contrast of surface
and materials, planes in space - these have rather specific and
simple expression with regard to the setting unit, within these
expanse and enclosure should be readily grasped. Skylines are the
lines of maximum visual contrast within the landscape. Usually they
are a product of ridge or shoulder lines of landforms with solidity
seen against the fluid color of sky. There is the fundamental contrast between dark and light, solid and atmosphere. The observer's
position within the bounds of the unit and upon the earth's surface

should give emphasis to this earth-sky contrast. (Whitman, 1968).

Obviously, sky edges or silhouettes may also involve plants and

water, as well as landmass edge.

Fig. 16 - The visual boundary between two setting
units, Wind River, Wyoming

The contour edges of closer planes of land or plants seen

against more distant backgrounds are not normally the strong lines

that are sky silhouettes. Yet the overlapping planes of one surface

seen against another is a fundamental way whereby distance is sensed.

(Gibson, 1950). With this is the development of aerial perspective

which involves the blue or grey color changes and simplifications

of detail that are seen in the distance, as compared to those sharper

colors and details of the foreground. Indeed, the overlapping planes and the blueness of distance have been so generally recognized as to give the name to the Blue Ridge and the Great Smokies. Overlapping land surfaces and the haze of distance can be one of the outside boundaries of the setting unit.

The edges of lakes or streams as central elements within the setting unit involve a contrast similar in contrast to that of the skyline. While water surface is more expressive of expanse than of limitation, yet edges of water against land, water against plants, and water against sky are relationships of strong contrasts. (Moore, 1957; Cullen, 1953). These kinds of contrast edges may often provide water emphasis showing a central or commanding position within the unit.

The edges of vegetation or forest margins, particularly as expressed through junction of dissimilar and contrasting plant types, can help in a subtle way to show the margins of a setting unit. They can as well demark important characteristics within a setting unit. In the West the grassland or sage cover contrasted against Douglas fir could be very characteristic of a particular region's setting unit. In the Appalachian Ridge a continuous and unbroken hardwood vegetation cover would not be expected to differentiate one unit from another. Demarcation of the presence of water within a unit may be more than water itself, being the combined visual product of plants and water together. Cottonwoods along the Platte River say "water" just as do birch and hemlock along the Allagash. The pond cypress islands of Florida in early spring green seen against

pines or hardwood also give a sign that can be characteristic for a
setting unit. In their unobtrusive way the changes of vegetation can
help show the margins or boundaries of a setting unit.

Enclosure

While it is arbitrary and at times difficult to separate the idea
of enclosure from landform to which it especially relates, enclosure
includes visual relationships at various scales and with diverse
vertical-horizontal proportions among parts (Lewis, 1968). Two
different kinds of enclosure may be first noted: those of basins
associated with lakes and those of corridors associated with streams.
Yet, of course, the two are not self exclusive. The surroundings of
the Finger Lakes in Upper New York are more suggestive of linear
corridors than they are of more usual saucer-like lake basins.

Fig. 17 - Strong corridor enclosure by steep rock faces,
Clark Fork of the Yellowstone River

Morainal lakes or ponds in Minnesota or Wisconsin are most apt
to have enclosure expressed by plant and tree margin, or else the low
rolling mounds of glacial till soils. (See Fig. 10). So also would
be Florida's lakes on the coastal plain show minimum enclosure due to
the proportions found between the expanse of the water body and the
height of surrounding trees. While characteristic of given areas
or regions, these simple and regular basins while displaying as much
unity as any water body, they will lack the visual interest that would
come out of the variation associated with irregular basins and irregular
enclosure. Cirque lakes in any alpine area, while perhaps simple in
their outline, will normally be distinguished by the massively impressive
enclosure about them consisting of scree slopes, rock surfaces, or high
towering ridges above the water. Thus, their distinction comes largely
from enclosure.

Shasta Lake in California while suffering the disadvantages of
drawdown edges (Jackson, 1970) is a good example of a highly irregular
basin with many arms that correspond directly with the enclosure of
numerous high faced spurs. (See Fig. 15). Having the linear character
of its being a former stream valley with many side tributaries, the
width of each part of the lake is nowhere far or distant from steep
enclosing faces. From the irregularity of such a basin sufficient
variety is developed so that individual arms can be identified as consisting of waterscape units, subdivisions within the larger setting
unit in this case. The important visual relationship between the water

body as a flat surface is that maximum contrast is developed as steeper, more sheer, and higher enclosure is found adjacent to the water plane (Research Planning and Design, 1968). In its simplest terms this is the contrast between vertical and horizontal lines with maximum vividness or strength of image. (Zube and Dega, 1964).

For setting units which are described as elongated (or corridors) their side to side or cross section enclosure may be described as symmetrical or asymmetrical.

52

Fig. 18 - Symmetrical enclosure

Fig. 19 - Asymmetrical or "single sided" enclosure

Where space has been carved from horizontal formations or from homogeneous material, the expectation will be of nearly equal enclosing faces. On the upper Potomac for example, the nearly equal left and right sides are further made similar by their continuous hardwood cover. This aspect of a setting unit could be called placid and consistent though tending to be lacking in variety except as geological irregularities may be encountered. Lack of variety in the setting unit enclosure may, however be rescued by variety present in the waterscape unit or units found within the setting. Asymmetrical corridors, the products associated with inclined, folded, or broken formations will tend toward the development of greater interest within the setting unit enclosure.

Fig. 20 - Asymmetrical corridor associated with inclined
strata, vegetation pattern variations, Gros
Ventre slide lake, Wyoming

The Gros Ventre River is associated with an inclined structure which sets one long and relatively easy sloping face of enclosure opposite that of a highly steepened and irregular face on the opposite side. From the stream bottom one enclosure skyline is close at hand, the other two or three times as far away. The facial angle variations are further elaborated upon by differences in amount and patterns of vegetative cover.

Whether or not a corridor may be described as symmetrical, the presence of water close in to one side and more distant from the opposite side will move in the direction of inconsistency or what might be termed "single sided" enclosure. The Shenandoah River meanders near Strasborg, Virginia demonstrates this. With one abrupt face and ridge line within a half mile of the meander centers, while on the opposite site the ridge line is some five or six miles away. This apparently single-sided enclosure could also be exemplified in the case of the lake with water horizon on one side with shore-setting enclosure close and abrupt on the other.

The ends of corridor spaces, whether fluvial or lacustrine, may be characterized as either open or closed. With the end open as a portal,there may yet be the distant ending characterized by the in-distinction or haziness of aerial perspective. With terminal closure due either to a bend in the corridor or the presence of a projecting spur, the end surface becomes important as a focal area since the lines of the corridor all converge toward the focal face. The nature of that surface assumes special importance in the distinction of the setting unit and its enclosure.

While there is enclosure or visual screen from forest edges,
there is also the maximum enclosure to be suggested by overhead tree
canopy. Although canopy as related to waterbodies is a more special
concern of the waterscape unit, it can have a particular effect
within the setting unit. For the small scale stream, a total tree
canopy may effectively hide the presence of water surfaces within
the bigger unit. For settings in flattened or rolling country the
overlapping canopy at water's edge can also effectively blanket the
presence of water. While this screening of water is but factual within
many settings, it places water in a subordinate role within the setting
unit, working against quality expression.

Fig. 21 - Enclosure seen as forest cover and tree edges

Landform

While the characteristic forms of land have been suggested in
the discussion of boundary definition and enclosure, a brief review
of landform patterns would be useful in establishing a sense of
landscape character. As a simplification, the setting unit can be
characterized as occuring within one of three different visual forms:
1) flattened or continuous and easily sloping surfaces 2) hill
formations which roll or continue in undulating order and 3) mountainous forms which are rough, irregular or tend toward irregularity.
More limited specifications can be drawn in particular cases and no
setting unit can be expected to embrace more than one reasonably
consistent landform expression.

Flattened landscape forms can be encountered on flood plains
or large alluvial fans, on coastal plains and interior lowlands, or
on flattened basins or upon upland plateaus. With an emphasis of
placid horizontally, enclosure elements will often be those of vegetation or low lying ridges and with minimum or indistinct definition
of setting unit. Indeed under these circumstances, the setting unit
may, because of its lack of distinction, give way to the waterscape
unit - that unit which is clearly related to water.

Hill forms represent a continuum running from smooth and consistently rounded surfaces to broken and inconsistent yet undulate
ridges. Piedmont areas as transitional forms between flatland and
upper mountainous terrain are one expression. Plateau country and
continental glaciation can also be characterized for presence of

rounded and undulate hill character.

Hill landforms may also be characterized as larger in scale or smaller with pattern derived from coarse grained to finer drainage. Larger scale combinations tend to be the more dynamic. The setting unit in larger, steeper hills takes on an intermediate character approaching aggressive linear angularity of mountainous terrain. Visual quality of setting units become more positive and vivid as landform becomes more definite.

Fig. 22 - A combination of hill and mountain landforms within a setting unit, Granite Creek, Wyoming

Mountains and those aggregations of mountain forms collected into ranges represent the most dynamic expression of landform. Forceful products of volcanism and glaciation, they demonstrate

upthrust verticality and angularity, posing visually exciting dimensions
or limits. Setting units in such environments offer the greatest of
contrast to be seen related to water. Mountain lakes with their
characteristically flat surface plane can be seen in maximum contrast
to surrounding verticals and nearby angular ridge lines. (See. Fig. 6).
This is a source of visual vividness associated with the combination.
In a somewhat different fashion, youthful streams in mountainous situations are characterized by the amount of variation and contrast that
they carry. Quick changes from smooth water to fast water, from
meanders to cascades, or the presence of waterfalls are to be expected.
This variety in water character is as much a part of mountain terrain
pattern as it is of water to conform to the pattern. (U.S. Army Corps
of Engineers, USDI, USDA, 1969; Research Planning and Design Associates,
1967).

Vegetation Patterns

Vegetation patterns within the setting unit involve the juxtaposition of four different types of cover or surface: 1) tree cover -
either broadleaf or coniferous, 2) scrub cover, 3) grassland, 4) barren or mineralized/soil surface apparently bare of vegetative components.
Each of the cover types/surface types consist essentially of a continuous
or generally repetitive textural body. Pattern itself develops at the
edge and margins or the junctions of these differing textural surfaces.
These connective margins between or among dissimilar vegetation types
may be categorized and set down in order of their relative visual
strength. In order, these margins are: 1) butt, 2) transitional,

3) digitate, and 4) diffuse. The butt edge is sharp and positive

in the linear contrast between two differing covers. Grassland

adjoining coniferous trees would demonstrate this kind of strong

meeting. A transitional edge involves a double butt junction or the

inclusion of a third element between two dissimilar types. Brush or

Fig. 23 - Sharp, butt edges between contrasting plant
types - a strong vegetative pattern, Shoshone
National Forest, Wyoming

shrubby materials intermediate between grassland and coniferous forest

would be representative. It should be a distinct edge but somewhat

softer than the straight butt edge. The digitate edge is one with

interlocked fingers which may assume a number of visual guises --

from strong and clear contrast to fuzzy and gradual merging margins.

Stringers of trees meeting barren faces, sometimes broken off into clumps or even drifting off to individuals, represent this kind of edge. The diffuse edge can be expected to be soft and gradual in the gradual joining together of plants which offer no marked contrast between or among one another. If, for example, a number of different kinds of hardwood trees are brought together in a diffuse joint, the generalized visual effect would be little different from that of a continuous and undifferentiated vegetation type.

A setting unit in the enclosure of a stream valley in central Idaho near the Salmon River indicates the kind of varietal strength that can be contributed by strong vegetative pattern.

Fig. 24 - Rich and varied vegetation patterns as part
of a setting unit, Challis National Forest, Idaho

Butting it in the bottom is the clumpy texture of riparian willow although no water is apparent. On the south facing slope, the pattern is one of mixed pine stringers, aspen groupings or groves marking

moist sites, and sagebrush-grassland surfaces filling the interstices.

It is a highly interesting surface because of its variations and

comparison to the more somber continuity of the north facing slope,

a generally consistent cover of Douglas Fir and lodgepole pine

making up an unbroken surface. Differences of orientation in other

Rocky Mountain setting units, or for that matter, those in the southern

Blue Ridge can produce such variations. Vegetative pattern variations

can well occur in hardwood country because of seasonal changes - winter

to spring, spring to summer, summer to fall, each a temporary pattern

more distinct than that expected in continuous conifer types.

Apart from the vegetation patterns that can give vividness or

placidity to the faces of setting enclosure, there is the special visual

function of the plant communities which align themselves with streams

or lakes (See Figs. 25 and 26). In the Oregon Coast Range, the lines

of bigleaf maple following stream edges can be expected to stand out

against backgrounds of fir and spruce. Even if water itself is under

the canopy, the stream alignment will be well marked. As autumn exerts

itself, the yellow color of cottonwoods along the Rio Grande will

flag the line of the watercourse standing out against the contrast

of surrounding scrub. Other seasonal changes can also bring out this

kind of plant - water relationship in heightened visibility.

Fig. 25 - Cottonwood rows marking a western watercourse

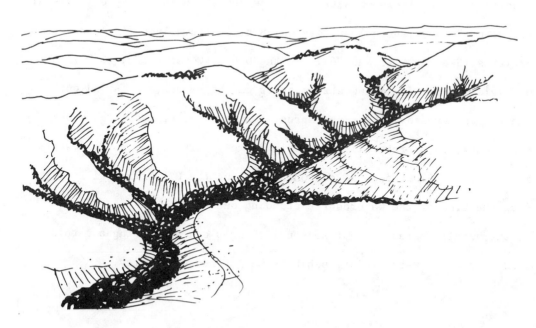

Fig. 26 - Riparian vegetation conforming to
the drainage pattern in rolling hills

Features

At the scale of the setting unit, features are those individual "things" which stand out in their surroundings. Like features anywhere they will be recognized by their isolation, by contour distinction size or scale domination, or by strong surface variations. (Litton, 1968). Easily recognized by the ways in which they contrast with their surroundings, individual features are derived from earth or landform, from conspicuous water expression, or eminent tree groupings. Frequently, the recognition of a particular feature will be the source of a place name.

Distinctive geological formations will be recognized by their prominence of outline silhouette or color in opposition to their background. (U.S. National Park Service, 1968; U.S. Army Corps, USDI, USDA, 1969). To name a few - there are peaks and pinnacles, cliffs and palisades, domes, escarpments, and outcrops. They may be found anywhere within a setting unit making an obvious part of the enclosing facade. They may appear most effectively as the focal terminals to a unit. (See Fig. 27). A palisade or group of palisades, such as those on the Hudson, offer the special distinction of vertical faces being seen as intersecting with the horizontal surface of water - a powerful contrast. Side canyon junctions with streams or lakes may well be the sites where exposed outcrops or cliffs are revealed. Hard rock features are given emphasis by association with water.

Fig. 27 - Mountain peaks displayed as focal features,
Castle Peak, White Cloud Range, Idaho

Waterfalls constitute the most obvious source of water features
and they are relatively rare in the landscape. (See Fig. 29). But
a waterfall being a special kind of fast moving water at some disjointed
point in the water course, also shows up because of its contrast to
what may be more usual water movement above and below it. A cascade
or chute, such as the Great Falls on the Potomac, stand out because
of their dissimilarity from upstream and downstream waters. Additionally, the knickpoint, plunge pool and immediate gorge or cavern enclosure usual about a fall reinforce the visual impact of the whole
feature. Quite an opposite kind of contrast may also be that of still
and deep, dark pools which are displayed against faster moving or white
water above and below them.

While water features are as much a part of the waterscape unit as they are of the setting unit, they tend to have a subordinate position within the setting unit because of proportional size related to landscape. They are not apt to be more dominant elements within the waterscape unit.

Plant features are particularly those made up of individual trees of note or tree groupings. They are the most subtle features that may occur within a setting unit. While individual trees are important as single isolated features, they may be difficult to identify and yet more difficult to see with ease. The present "tallest redwood in the world" is not the same one that was for years identified in that way. The oldest bristlecone pine, measured as the oldest living tree on earth, is not even identified for its own safety. More practically, tree features are apt to be those groves - groupings of trees - that have some joint distinction constituting such contrasting collections as the Sierra Redwood - Mariposa grove, or an old-age hardwood cove in the Ozarks. Despite their quiet assertiveness, tree grove features can determine high quality for setting units. (Morisawa & Murie,1969; Nighswonger,1970).

A single feature, regardless of what it may be, can be thought of as a central element having a sphere of influence. This can aid in the identity of a setting unit and provide a means of recognition, not infrequently going so far as to provide a name.

Human Impacts

There is perhaps no situation in which the impact of human use is more significant than as it impinges upon the landscape of the

setting unit. As the Potomac River task force report (1968) notes:
"Development of the wrong kind can disastrously affect its scenic
quality."

Potential development appears in such diverse forms as nature
trails, resorts, urbanization or dam building. It is rare that full
and complete design conceptions for these facilities are appropriately
visualized or well guided. The usual accumulation of partial solutions,
made with little or no real reference to the setting landscape can be
expected to degrade quality.

As with the water element of the setting unit, development
should be built to respond directly to native landscape characteristics.
(Smith, 1969; Gill, 1969; Ingham, 1969; Gibberd, 1967). Or it may also
succeed with clear cut contrast (Crowe & Browne, 1959).

Water Expression

While it has been essential to discuss water under the heading of landscape since it is inseparable from the land which contains it, there are three general factors which suggest ways in which water can be related to its setting unit. They are: 1) its prominence, 2) its continuity, and 3) its transition. Additionally, there is the human impact involving water surface and its immediate edge.

Prominence

This concerns the relative dominance or subordinance of water as found and as expressed within the setting. For the lake within its basin, the normal expectation is that water will appear dominant because of the large proportion of the general flat that is given over to water coverage. Yet as old age takes over, upstream filling by sediment and the encroachment by vegetation proceeds with water surface steadily diminishing over time until it disappears. The irregular basin with steeper side slopes can be expected to contain a more conspicuous and dominating water surface than that of a regular containment (Crowe & Browne, 1959). This can be attributed not only to the outline shape, but also to the contrast between the horizon plane of water surface seen in opposition to angular surrounding shore elements. For the lake with more regular basin, a flatter site is implied with more obscure sense of edge; there is diminishment of contrast because of similarity between horizontal water plane and adjacent shore or setting.

68

A

B

Fig. 28 A-B - Comparative prominence of water surface in the same
            lake setting unit - the younger and older lake

While marked contrast between waterscape and setting has the
potential for visual interest, the isolation of one from another must
be assessed as a lowering of quality. (Maryland, 1970). Variety
within the elements of transition should be marks of quality not only
through visual linkage but also ease or difficulty of physical access
as well - the two enhancing one another (University of Massachusetts,
1967; Craighead & Craighead, 1962; Nighswonger, 1970).

Fig. 29 - Tree screened transition between water
and the backshore

For fluvial expression of water, the volume of water and its
surface turbulence as seen within its setting enclosure should be
an index to its relative visual importance. Water in the younger
landscape can be expected to be more conspicuous as it seeks
adjustment to its surroundings. While the activity of the more
youthful stream surface will give it a more vivid impression, its
containment within a precipitous landscape may reduce its visibility.[*]
As the meanders of maturity develop, the total length of the stream
is increased and presumably it may offer increased opportunity for
more water surface to be revealed. Yet, meanders are apt to be but
simple repetitions and they can be expected to be accompanied by
screening vegetation. As riparian vegetation develops, perhaps
including that on braids and islands, good opportunities for
observation of water will begin to diminish. So a dilemma is at work.
Active and turbulent water, even if present in relatively lesser
amounts, will tend to be more prominent in its setting than may be
larger amounts of more calm water.

To return to the shore or the boundaries about water bodies,
the matter of prominence may be due to more advantageous viewing
opportunities rather than the actual amount of water present (Research
Planning and Design Associates, 1968). The flatter landscape tends to
diminish the importance of horizontal water surface through perspective foreshortening. The steeper and more irregular site,

[*] In the Smokies the French Broad cuts a deeper valley and is flanked
by higher mountains. But there the river is shallow and narrow, a
small stream practically hidden by the scale of the mountains. The
Hudson's relative breadth creates river scenery of an unequalled
scale. (Boyle, 1969)

whether in relation to lake or stream, should offer more opportunities for viewing and at the same time will provide a visual sense of more actual water surface because of better and more varied viewing positions (Lewis, 1968). Higher observer positions will enhance water prominence.

Water features have been discussed, but it should be reiterated that their presence - special segments visually differentiated from their surroundings and also from upstream and downstream counterparts - can be expected to have a dominating effect. They especially represent the factor of prominence even though their visibility from a distance or from many points within a setting unit may be limited.

Fig. 30 - The waterfall as a feature and expression of prominence, Germania Falls, Challis National Forest, Idaho

Continuity

Continuity is particularly concerned with the relationship
between waterscape units and a setting unit. For a stream at one time
in its stage of life, a waterscape unit might consist of a series of
meander sets each joined with swifter water or rapids between. If
the beginning and end of the setting unit happened to coincide with
such a waterscape unit, the two would reinforce one another in direct
fashion. This represents a clearcut expression of continuity. Several
waterscape units could well be found to exist within a single setting
unit. This combination might consist, for example, of a meander unit,
a turbulent cascade unit and a laminar flow unit all within a relatively
large or perhaps irregular setting. Continuity would largely accrue
from the setting itself while variety would develop from the differences
within the contained waterscape units. In yet another set of comparisons,
a waterscape unit consisting of a long sinuous laminar flow might well
embrace several setting units (See Fig. 21). While an uninterrupted
and continuous type of flow is certainly a continuity and serves
unification well, it suggests that visual interest is more apt to come
from the setting unit than from the waterscape.

While lakes tend to make their own continuity through expanse of
unbroken surface, the simple basin shape is apt to describe a single
and coincident setting and waterscape unit together. As irregularity
develops, isolated arms or island shielded bays should be identified
as waterscape units. Yet the continuity lies with the total water
surface and with the larger setting about the shore.

Transition

Transition is concerned with shore linkage between water and its
setting as well as setting to waterscape unit relationships. Landform
at the backshore edge may range from vertical face to near horizontally -
abrupt to gradual transition into setting. (Zube and Dega, 1964)
Involved are both the way the shore joins the water and the
nature of vegetation as it forms a link between land and water.

For the shallow lake   sited   within a flattened basin, including backshore vegetation growing in horizontal lines, transition is
characterized as repetition of similarities. While unified it is yet
monotonous, lacking variety and interest. (See Fig. 14). Transitional
variation, a positive quality, can come from a combination of backshore
vegetation and plants with their feet in the water. A pond in Florida
with bald cypress invading the water, is a simple display of transition
made by horizontal and vertical lines together, a combination enhanced
by adjacent sand beach shore.

With the shore constituting a vital point of linkage between the
water body and the setting, it may actually make a separation. Such
a barrier may be both physical and visual. The transparency of the
space between bald cypress about the Florida pond, must be assessed
as more desirable than a bull proof thicket. So also with gorge walls
or palisades, while visually dynamic especially as seen across the
water or from some access pocket, they may have the disadvantage of
cutting off the water body from its larger landscape. The flat and
open shore on one side is ideally contrasted to a palisade edge on the
offshore - a vivid possibility for either stream or lake.

Human Impacts

While impacts of human use and activities at the level of the
setting unit are discussed in another section, several generalized
observations may be made. Human impacts are modifiers which may be
either in opposition to or in sympathy with the natural conditions and
visual composition of the unit. Development can have the effect of
strengthening the native characteristics either by conforming or
repeating characteristics or they may also succeed with suitable
contrast. Developments could succeed because of their small scale
in relation to the setting, or they could fail because of their being
oversized for the setting. A conservative but useful design goal for
rural or wildland conditions would be that of exerting a minimum of
apparent influence upon the setting unit. Under urban conditions
such as those observable in Stockholm's water edge parks or at Lake
Geneva, carefully and well designed man-made margins and facilities
are in complete sympathy with much modified waterbodies. What may
be called appropriate design needs to be put into context of both place
and intensity of use.

WATERSCAPE UNIT

The waterscape unit is defined by the combination of two mutually interdependent expressions: the water element and the shore element. The shore and water depend upon each other and reflect each other's condition. (U.S. Dept. of Interior & the Fed. Interdept. Task Force on the Potomac, 1968). Visual dominance of a waterbody or unified segments of it occurs as parts stand out in contrast to the parent body. The nature of water in contrast to land as a solid is the source of its visual dominance, yet it can be true that the shore, because of area and expanse, may well transcend the area or expanse of water present. The extent and configuration of water as a body in the landscape is normally defined by the shore outline. An exception occurs as waterbodies are large enough to form their own horizon - observable in bodies over three wide miles as the viewer stands at the water's edge. Important to the definition of the waterscape unit is that the observer is assumed to be on the water or close by its edge. This choice of observer position lays stress on the importance of water itself as well as its immediate shore margin.

Relationships between the waterscape unit and the setting unit may vary from separation and complete isolation to visually open or coincident existence. A series of waterscape units may be found within one setting or a waterscape unit may be so long as to link up a series of setting units. This particular unit is no different from the other two in that its boundaries may be sharp and distinct or they may be hazy and difficult to discern.

The Water Element

The classification system considers the visual expression of the water element to be a product of five factors: space, movement, appearance, aquatic environment and evidence of human contact. The first three factors are especially stressed in this section.

Spatial Expression and Edge

One of the most distinctive and striking characteristics of water is its uniform coverage of an area. It is seen as a continuous surface within spatial bounds that occupies an area on the land. The space occupied by the water surface can be described by the dimensions of its size and its shape. Both external and internal edges define water shape. First, a particular shape is determined by its external edge - the land that encloses or outlines the water body and second, by the internal edge - land that is surrounded by the water body. (See Fig. 31).

The water surface shape usually assumes what can be called a fluvial or lacustrine definition. The spatial form of a stream body is primarily linear, determined by the flow and channel characteristics. This directional flow is described as a path across the land. The path can normally be recognized as having an apparent pattern and there are four: braids, meanders, sinuous and straight reaches. (Leopold and Wolman, 1957; Schumm, 1963). Sinuous, straight, and meander patterns, and their transitional forms, come out of the two external edges or shorelines which give visual demarkation. The braid pattern is formed by internal shape of water surface because of bars and islands as well

in addition to the external definition of the water course edges. (See
Fig. 32).

Fig. 31 - External shore edges and internal island
edges outline the water body

The overall exterior shape of a lake body can be characterized
as irregular or regular, a comparative relationship to simplicity or
complexity of geometric outline. Oval or round lakes such as Lake
Tahoe or Crater Lake can be compared to the contrast with irregular
ones such as Lake Mead or Lake-of-the-Woods, Minnesota. Smaller
lakes and those with simple outlines can be identified as having but
single waterscape units unless variations are induced by factors such
as microclimates or vegetation changes. The lake with complex shape,
because of embayments, arms or islands, can be assumed to represent a
collection of different waterscape units. The apparent shape and the

space that a lake occupies is thus defined not only by the outline of its shore but by the internal expression and shoreline of insular features - islands, islets, bars, or isolated rocks. To the degree that irregular shape represents a form of variety, higher quality should normally accrue to the more complex form. (See Fig. 6)

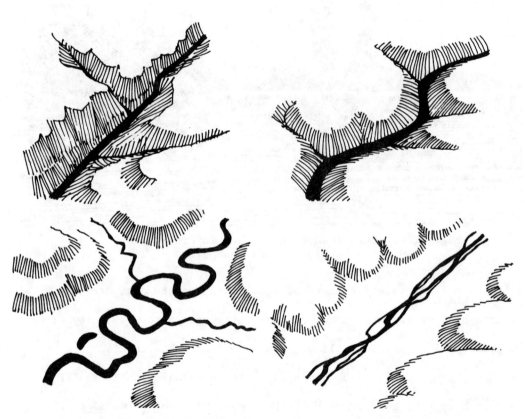

Fig. 32 - Four basic stream patterns: straight, sinuous, meander, and braid

While size expressed as square footage or perhaps dimensions of width and length are easily assembled statistics about a water body, they will say but little about quality.[*] The sense of size or the scale relationship between a river or water body and its adjoining shores is most realistically due to configuration and especially to complexity of shape. The large but simple lake seen from a single vantage point, seen completely, will not gain much distinction because of its size. A sinuous lake with many embayments and projecting points can be expected to provide a sense of large size through the gradual revealing of its parts over time. (Thiel, 1961). Visual mystery is coupled with the observer's movement as the whole is unveiled. It has been traditional in Japanese landscape design to conceal some part of a water body so it is never wholly visible from any one viewing place. (Kassler, 1968). A negative aspect of size has to do with fluctuation of water surface. (U.S. BOR, 1970); Jackson, 1970). Increases or decreases in the level of surface may mean the inundation or loss of native shoreline advantages or, in recession, the overemphasis of a mediocre shore edge. (Coppedge and Gray, 1967).

Movement and Features

Movement is probably the single most exciting and vivid quality associated with water. It may be the physical function of gravity descent, wind, or the two in combination. Gravity descent is equated to stream flow; wind driven waves and movement are primarily lake phenomena.

---

[*] 'The size of the lake seems to make only slight difference in the value of the property surrounding it. Property values do not increase consistently with each acre of lake surface. " (David and Lord, 1969).

Water movement in a stream course can be described as a combination of disturbed surfaces consisting of falling and turbulent characteristics and surfaces apparently undisturbed by flow. The most obvious kind of surface disturbance is represented by a vertical waterfall; the least apparent is that of seemingly horizontal laminar flow. Between these two extremes are a wide range of falling and turbulent forms: chutes, cascades, boils, rollers, rapids, ripples, and their combination in infinite variety. The visually demanding quality of water movement which produces vivid images is largely attributable to the contrast between the joining of disturbed and undisturbed water surfaces. (Leopold, 1968; Dearinger, 1968). The comparison is then made between rapid water and placid. (Nighswonger, 1970).

Fig. 33 - Fast moving water, a source of vivid quality

When moving contrast is marked enough, water features will emerge as isolated elements. (See Fig. 30). While there is a tendency to identify waterfalls and chutes as features, they may as readily be pools of quiet water. Water movement features, as to qualities of richness, also depend heavily upon their immediate shore housing. Lakes, if they are visually distinctive, are apt to be features.

Fig. 34 - The still pool as a feature, seen in
contrast to white water

Other discussion of these isolated feature compositions will be
found under the Setting Unit description.

Wind as a factor in water movement is directly dependent upon
the fetch of the water body. The visual dominance of wind waves can
be expected to increase in accordance with the fetch (size) of a lake
or perhaps with its long dimension in particular alignment to wind
direction or gap. While sizeable waves will occur only on larger
bodies of water, wind streaking or rippling can noticeably alter the
surface of any lacustrine body or large river. Waves, streaks, or
rippling also constitutes a form of contrast to quiet or reflective
surfaces. While wind represents a temporary factor, it is a source

of apparent vitality, bolstering what may be called water personality.[*]

Appearance

The appearance of water in its place is a composite factor of
its fluidity or its liquidness, its clarity and color, and its capacity
to reflect light and images.

The fact of a water's fluidity is tuned to its capacity to assume
the form of its container - the shore which arrests movement - and
for its capacity to float or suspend materials. Relative clarity is
a simple and positive mark of quality. The more clear water may be,
the more apt it is to command attention. And the more it is apt to
be called beautiful. Clearness does permit a deeper and detailed
view of bottom characteristics, a visual distinction that Thoreau
commented about at Walden. If the bottom is pleasing in its composition,
including boulders or boulders and sand, then that view is an added
dimension to aesthetic quality. However, those lakes in the world that
are especially clear, such as Crater Lake or Lake Tahoe, are described
less in terms of their clarity and more in terms of color, such as sky
blue or turquoise. The combination of transparency coupled with color
is a particularly striking visual combination.

Color of any water body is obviously one of its chief attributes,
whether that color is rusty red from suspended sediments or turquoise
from clarity and the combined light reflection of sky and water

---

[*] "On land only the trees and grass wave, but the water itself is
rippled by the wind. I see where the breeze dashes across it by
streaks or flashes of light." Thoreau, "The Ponds", Walden.

84

together.[*] Because water color is a combination of a number of different
conditions (bottom composition, clarity, incidence of light, dissolved
and suspended material) no accurate classification for comparative
evaluation has been developed. However, some general color groups and
turbidity-clarity ranges could be developed for water to provide an
index to visual quality.

Transparent depth of water as a liquid and its surface with smooth
sheen can act in concert to provide reflective qualities. Among its
other attributes water has been described as nature's mirror of the
landscape, on which inverted images appear. Or the shimmering light
of the sun of the moon are seen in a secondary guise. Materials carried
on the surface, leaves in small streams, driftwood carried or deposited
at the shore are also reminders that water is liquid. "The lit river,
purling and eddying onward was spotted with recently fallen leaves,
some which are being carried around in eddies". Thoreau's Journals,
The River, 1963. The nature and amount of material carried by water,
whether suspended or on top, also offer a clue to quality level.

Aquatic Environment

Plants and animals that exist within the water column are considered to be components of the aquatic environment. While both are
subtle additions to the water itself, they provide or may provide
enrichment or they may provide a special kind of transition to the
edge. (U.S.F.W.P.C.A., 1968).

Aquatic vegetation - purely of the water such as lilies or reeds -

---

* "All our Concord waters have two colors at least, one viewed at
a distance, and another, more proper, close at hand." Thoreau,
"The Ponds", Walden.

are those visibly surrounded by water. They will not appear to be
an extension of shore vegetation so long as they do not merge with it
at the water line. If such plants cover the whole water surface, they
may be considered as visually degrading - as will merging with shore
originated plants so the whole contrast between water and land disappears. Aquatic vegetation will appear attractive only so long as
it is clearly related to water and does not confuse the land - water
contrast.

Fish, as the characteristic fauna of the aquatic environment, may
well be the reason for approaching water or being on it. Opportunities
to see anadromous fish jumping rapids, preparing redds or jamming small
tributaries are indeed visual bonuses. The usual amphibions - alligators,
turtles, and frogs: water birds - ducks, herons, geese; or water
mammals - beaver, otter, muskrats - all may at some time or place be
visible and give visual pleasure to the observer. Those situations
which encourage the sighting of fish or animals associated with the
water and shore are becoming rare enough so that suitable conditions
and environment need protection or development. This is still another
kind of variety which spells quality. The sight of animals in the
landscape are precise occurrences and should be recognized for their
capacity to produce vivid impressions.

Evidence of Human Impact - Water Element

Human impact evidence is generally attributable to either the
direct modification made in the flow or configuration of the water

body or else the visual presence of pollution. Channelization and
structural edge changes may not be disadvantageous though they tend
to be because of single purpose solutions which are monotonous and
thwart human use and pleasure. (U.S. BOR, 1969; Davidson, 1970).
Aspects of these changes are discussed under Section III.

Pollution evidence, which includes discoloration, floating debris,
the presence of slicks or an unnatural degree of turbidity, all presumably affect the aquatic environment and the plants and animals which
reside there. These, of course, must be considered as degradations
in quality. (Willeke, 1968; U.S. FWPCA, 1968). Visual evidence of
pollution is not superficial. It may well be the cause instituting
water quality controls fully as much as the fear that health might be
threatened by pollution. (Kneese, 1967).

The Shore Element

The waterscape classification framework considers the visual element of the shore to be the product of five factors: edge definition, space, edge features, riparian environment, and evidence of human impact. The shore is a platform of human activity. It is the place from which water may be best seen and often best enjoyed; it should be recognized for values that rival that of adjoining water. While the shore has its own attributes, for better or for worse, its essential worth is dependent upon its water association. (Tennessee, Dept. of Cons., 1970).

Edge Definition - Vertical and Longshore

The visual edge of any water body is composed of both horizontal and vertical definition. The horizontal - or long shore definition - is that which runs parallel with the water edge. The vertical defi- nition - or cross shore demarcation - is perpendicular to the junction between land and water. Shore types prove to be difficult to categorize because they compound variety through both longshore and cross-shore variations. (Michigan State Univ., 1968; Zube and Dega, 1964). But differentiation by shore types can be the way whereby a waterscape unit is defined.

All vertical or cross shore definitions, when viewed across a foreground of water, can be described in terms of the form they present. They are the evidence of particular kinds of transition between water and land. This cross sectional junction can be depicted either as an abrupt face or gradual face or some combination of the two. An abrupt face could be characterized as a cliff, a bluff or palisade, bulkhead, hedgerow of trees, or forest edge.

Fig. 35 - Palisades or gorge walls as abrupt edge
definition of the shore

The gradual face would have a low and easy slope such as beach, marsh,
marsh-to-meadow verge, or low profile levee. As in any attempt to
categorize, there is no absolute separation between those shore
faces which are abrupt and those which are gradual. The terms are
used to describe the relative strength of the vertical shore relationship. Transition between the shore edge and water edge are thus
defined in terms of contrast. Two extremes of the shore junction
would be a blended edge such as aquatic vegetation bleeding into
riparian reeds all on a flat plane as compared to a striking contrast
edge such as a palisade that rises directly from the water.

Fig. 36 - Adjacent contrasts in shore edge: vertical
outcrop barrier and open access under a shore grove

The longshore definition is a continuous one with no definable

beginning or end except as it comes out of the cross-shore changes.

Consideration of the longshore definition can be organized according

to the apparent shoreline enclosure of the water body. For most

streams the shores are seen as the opposing sides of the water

corridor. They may provide generous space or constriction. Lacus-

trine bodies tend to form a circular shore or a segmented one that

follows the basin space definition. Along large lakes and the

largest of the world's rivers, only one shoreline will be apparent

either because a water horizon may occur or distance will diminish

the importance of the far shore. An index to shore quality would include the symmetry or asymmetry created between the near and opposing shore; the degree of continuity or variation that each showed could be compared. Water itself can provide unity or continuity to be coupled to variation in the shore character. A stream that develops similar but opposing shoretypes along the edge will exhibit a form of symmetry that can be expected to stand in sharp contrast to expected irregularities of the surrounding setting.

Variations of shoretypes along one side of a corridor can be expected to display one of three conditions: 1) no apparent changes, 2) repetitive or alternating variation - producing a longshore pattern, 3) cross-shore variations which obscure longshore pattern development. Without apparent or conspicuous visual change, quality can be presumed to suffer from monotony. Recognizable repetition of a number of contrasting shoretypes should be equated to higher visual quality (Maryland, 1970). If variations are without some kind of apparent order - such as repetition or restatement - the effect may be one approaching chaos.

A basin longshore definition assumes a circular, self-closing outline. The shores are not often opposing as in the corridor definition, but appear as a single continuous encirclement of the water body. Opposing shores, though visible, may be too distant or disoriented from one another to make evident contrast. The single shore definition of large lakes and rivers assumes either that no opposing shore is visible or is so distant as to be diminished to scant visual importance. The same three conditions that described longshore variation of the corridor side are applicable to both the basin shore definition and the single shore definition.

Spatial Expression

The spatial expression is a function of the distance between opposing shores and the height of the vertical shore face. It is linked with edge definition. The waterscape's spatial enclosure will be expected to increase, becoming more conspicuous, as the ratio of the distance to the height decreases. Shore walls that form canyons, gorges, and ravines will create extreme enclosure and command attention. There is a degree of regional magnitude involved - what may be called an impressive gorge in one landscape unit might not be in another. (Cain, 1968). Low gradual slopes surrounding large lacustrine bodies will convey the impression of no enclosure and small likelihood of visual distinction. It can be expected that stream corridor shores will exhibit a higher degree of enclosure than lake basin or single shore definitions.

Edge Features

Edge features are vivid focal points displayed against background foil of the shore. They include rock outcrops associated with water-falls, side canyon bluffs, caves, and eccentric boulders and riparian accents. They are highlights or discontinuities which assume importance in their relationship to commonly encountered shores (USNPS, 1968). Such feature points - frequently linked to water features - often constitute the most memorable images along stream or lake margin. They may serve to characterize or overshadow the entire associated shore definition. They are marks of quality - true of features whenever they are encountered.

Fig. 37 - Edge feature - unusual outcrop shore with
ordinary backshore

Riparian Environment

Certain visual aspects of the riparian environment have been
discussed under Edge Definition above and with regard to Vegetative
Patterns in setting units. Linear demarkation of stream or lake
presence - especially with seasonal emphasis - is a major visual
function of shore zone plants. But at the level of the waterscape
unit there are a number of specific characteristics that may be noted.

Shore edge plants are most apt to make a special enclosure for
adjacent water. This will be the major space definition where the
cross shore profile is flattened - trees and associated plants assuming a dominant role. Where land form is strong - high banks, cliffs,
or canyon walls - wet zone plants will be transitional in form between
the water surface and the back-up land faces. (Brower, 1964). In the
transitional role, plants become subordinate in the whole composition.
Small "jewels" of plant composition may, of course, be found within
the transition zone. Where access is inhibited by plants which are
a barrier carried right to the water's edge, waterscape quality will
be degraded except for the user-viewer who is actually on the water.
Yet an open stand of riparian trees, making a transparent canopied space
adjacent to water can enhance the unit. (See Fig. 29). Such a grove
space can be a feature.

Apart from the gorge that may contain a riparian stringer in the
waterscape unit, an individual tree such as a single giant cottonwood
slong the Wind River or the North Platte could well mark the identification of a unit. Some waterscape units can be recognized as

distinct for the way in which a tree edge is reflected off the water
surface - some reaches of the Umpqua in Oregon show this.

Plants of the riparian zone are the least aggressive elements of
visual composition as they are compared to water and land forms. Yet
in some circumstances they are a substitute for the spatial functions
more dynamically produced by land faces. Beyond this they provide
visual enrichment that needs to be assessed in the identification
and evaluation of the waterscape unit. The presence of certain
animals that may be associated with the riparian zone is also a source
of additional diversity.

Fig. 38 - Cottonwood stringer as canopy marking a waterscape
unit, Challis National Forest, Idaho

Evidence of Human Impacts - Shore Element

For the waterscape unit, some description has been provided within the Water Element category above. Buildings, docks, excavation, and bridges represent the kind of impacts expected to act upon the shore environment. These are discussed in Section III.

INVENTORIES

Inventories of the water-landscape resource represent the need for documenting in a tangible and graphic way those components and relationships that portray the resource. While good intentions may exist for the protection and compatible use of native aesthetic characteristics found in water and landscape, it is unrealistic to expect that this can happen without convincing records. This special inventory with the purpose of portraying aesthetic characteristics depends upon the plotting of the visual components that have been discussed in the classification section.

It is important that this kind of visual survey record not be confused with a recreation inventory or one which has been convention- ally assembled in order to suggest particular kinds of land use potentials that may exist. While a visual landscape inventory may give implications for use and development - and should, - it must be perfectly clear that a land use potential survey is no substitute for a visual survey. This kind of confusion has existed in the past and presumably still exists. It is, of course, much easier to discover what land areas may be recreationally useful as compared to making records of landscapes for their differences of aesthetic quality. Failure to portray this kind of information has been influenced by the question of what to protray. It is our recommendation that certain distinctive aspects of what may be seen in water and landscape are reasonably easy to record and present in a useful document.

Although the inventory is an information base, it is not by
itself evaluative. Rather, it is factual, carries material which
is subject to evaluation and that will appear as supplementary to
the general instrument. However, since all possible items of inventory cannot be reasonably included, discretion is necessarily
applied as to what information is to be included. Since judgment
indicates that certain factors of lesser importance be omitted, it
also suggests that distinctive combinations of elements be recognized
and recorded.* This does initiate evaluative thinking.

Three levels of intensity or detail are implied by different
inventories which conform to the three already outlined units:
Landscape Unit, Setting Unit, or Waterscape Unit. Keeping in mind
that water is a key element, it is stressed that the concept of
unity is supported only the the inventory series which include whole
stream or lake systems from beginning to end. This idea is generally
portrayed in the landscape unit inventory; its use is directed toward integrative planning. More detailed records (still controlled
by the concept of unity) will be indicated in the setting unit and
waterscape unit which include the continuity of single streams or
connected lake bodies. The setting and waterscape inventories offer
more direct support to localized design and management decisions.

It is assumed to be critical that the basic inventory be put in
map form - a graphic record for a visual resource and one that can be

* Appendix C provides a listing of factors selected by other
investigators as basis for aesthetic quality evaluation.

related to physical plans and design. Examples are presented in
Appendix B. There will also be the need for secondary supporting
documentation, including narrative report, photographic samples,
diagrams, sketches, and evaluation tables.

Procedure and Field Work

While the starting point for an inventory will normally be a
topographic map at suitable scale for the unit to be considered, primary
dependence upon field reconnaisance is essential. There is no kind of
logic that suggests that it is possible to make a visual survey without
field work. In addition to topographic maps, those showing soils,
geological types, and vegetation types will prove useful as will air
photos. Since field work, in all practicality, will constitute a
sampling process, air photos can be most helpful in extending comprehensive coverage. Photo interpretation is also bolstered in
accuracy by field work samples.

For landscape unit surveys a small scale (large area) topographic map such as 1:250,000 scale (1 inch equals approximately 4
miles) would be appropriate. Reconnaissance by air with oblique
photo sampling and auto surface travel will be needed. Elements of
the inventory would include boundary types and major edges for the
unit, general physiographic form, surface terrain patterns, collective or large features, vegetation patterns, generalized water
presence and appearance, and cultural patterns. A detailed outline
checklist of inventory elements appropriate at this scale is placed
at the end of this section. (See Fig. 39,40,41.)

Inventory for the setting unit and the waterscape unit begins
with larger scale (smaller area) topographic maps such as 1:24,000
scale (1 inch equals 2,000 feet) or 1:62,500 (1 inch equals approximately 1 mile). The limits of the setting unit are defined as a
visual corridor or a visual envelope rough plotted in the field and
by use of cross sections. Boundaries are those within the confines
of enclosed space. For the setting unit, inventoriable items include those having to do with landscape character such as enclosure,
landform features and patterns, vegetation patterns and features.
Also for the setting, evidence of water character would include
factors of prominence, features, continuity of water and the lines
or visual ties between water and setting. Evidence of human impacts
would indicate access paths, structures concerned with activities and
facilities as well.

The waterscape inventory would be tied to the basic stream of
water body continuity and shore relationships. Under the water
element, factors, of movement, spatial expression, appearance, and
aquatic environment would be included. The shore element would include designation of edge or margin definitions, spatial expression,
features, and the shore environment. Human impacts would include
those that were specifically water related and shore related.

Evaluation forms can be developed for the purpose of summarizing
the presence, and numbers of items found in the landscape. Measure-
ments of widths, areas, or other quantifiable attributes of the

elements can be compared. This can provide a direct way of seeing how characteristics of variety may be analyzed and how distinctions may emerge. In their abstract simplification, such charts may not seem to speak strongly of aesthetic quality, but they do represent evidence to support logical qualitative analysis. For extensive and more complex comparisons, computerization of data should be considered.

Figure 39. Inventory Review Sheet--Landscape Unit

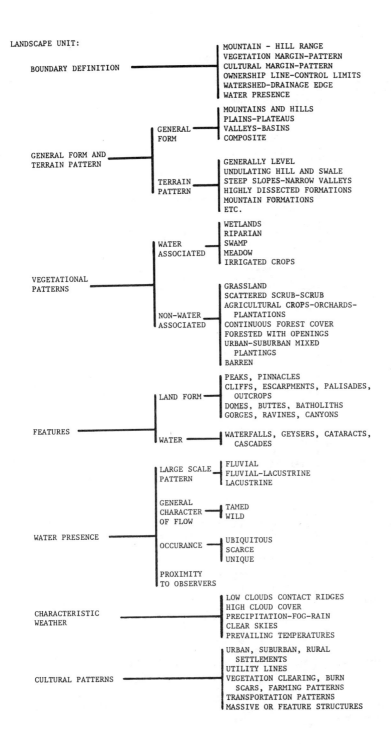

LANDSCAPE UNIT:

BOUNDARY DEFINITION
- MOUNTAIN - HILL RANGE
- VEGETATION MARGIN-PATTERN
- CULTURAL MARGIN-PATTERN
- OWNERSHIP LINE-CONTROL LIMITS
- WATERSHED-DRAINAGE EDGE
- WATER PRESENCE

GENERAL FORM AND TERRAIN PATTERN

GENERAL FORM
- MOUNTAINS AND HILLS
- PLAINS-PLATEAUS
- VALLEYS-BASINS
- COMPOSITE

TERRAIN PATTERN
- GENERALLY LEVEL
- UNDULATING HILL AND SWALE
- STEEP SLOPES-NARROW VALLEYS
- HIGHLY DISSECTED FORMATIONS
- MOUNTAIN FORMATIONS
- ETC.

VEGETATIONAL PATTERNS

WATER ASSOCIATED
- WETLANDS
- RIPARIAN
- SWAMP
- MEADOW
- IRRIGATED CROPS

NON-WATER ASSOCIATED
- GRASSLAND
- SCATTERED SCRUB-SCRUB
- AGRICULTURAL CROPS-ORCHARDS-PLANTATIONS
- CONTINUOUS FOREST COVER
- FORESTED WITH OPENINGS
- URBAN-SUBURBAN MIXED PLANTINGS
- BARREN

FEATURES

LAND FORM
- PEAKS, PINNACLES
- CLIFFS, ESCARPMENTS, PALISADES, OUTCROPS
- DOMES, BUTTES, BATHOLITHS
- GORGES, RAVINES, CANYONS

WATER
- WATERFALLS, GEYSERS, CATARACTS, CASCADES

WATER PRESENCE

LARGE SCALE PATTERN
- FLUVIAL
- FLUVIAL-LACUSTRINE
- LACUSTRINE

GENERAL CHARACTER OF FLOW
- TAMED
- WILD

OCCURANCE
- UBIQUITOUS
- SCARCE
- UNIQUE

PROXIMITY TO OBSERVERS

CHARACTERISTIC WEATHER
- LOW CLOUDS CONTACT RIDGES
- HIGH CLOUD COVER
- PRECIPITATION-FOG-RAIN
- CLEAR SKIES
- PREVAILING TEMPERATURES

CULTURAL PATTERNS
- URBAN, SUBURBAN, RURAL SETTLEMENTS
- UTILITY LINES
- VEGETATION CLEARING, BURN SCARS, FARMING PATTERNS
- TRANSPORTATION PATTERNS
- MASSIVE OR FEATURE STRUCTURES

Figure 40.   Inventory Review Sheet--Setting Unit

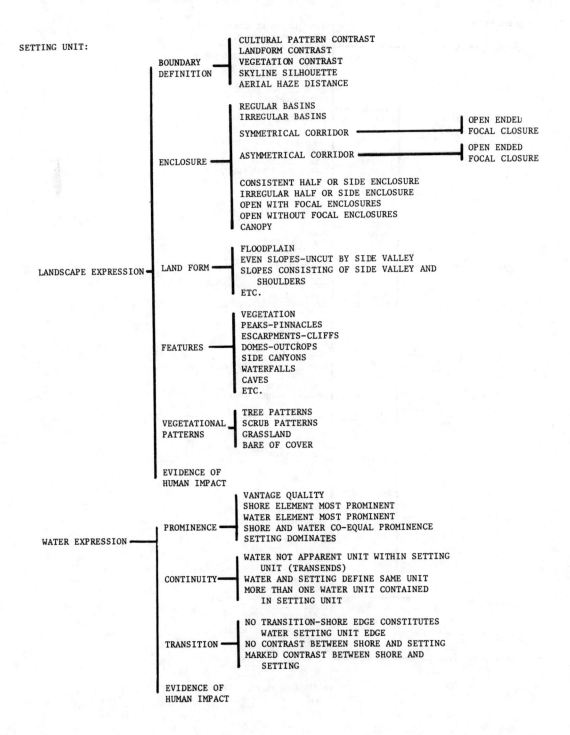

Figure 41. Inventory Review Sheet--Waterscape Unit

103

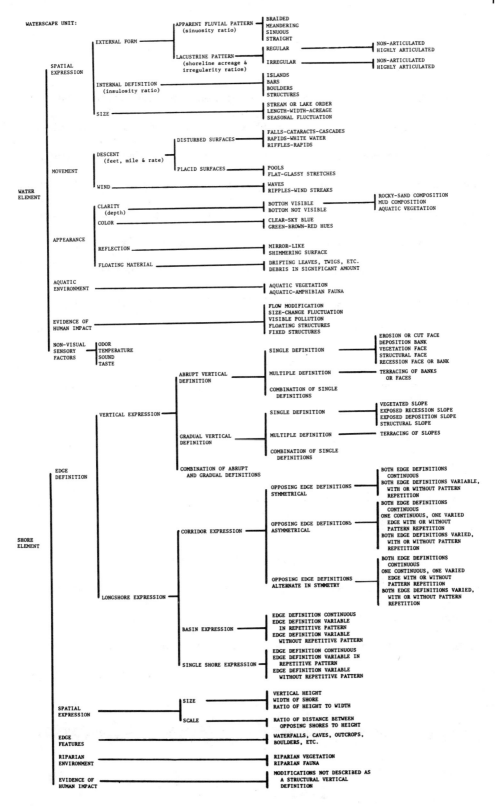

EVALUATION

In the Introduction the general components of aesthetic experience have been identified to consist of three parts. They are: the observer's state of mind, the context of observation, and environmental stimuli. Drawing upon the direct response of observer in the presence of environmental stimuli, we have indicated that there are three major sources of visual reaction within the landscape. Taking a limited scope, with the landscape considered to be made up primarily of landforms, water and plants, contemplation of these parts, if in proper combination, should produce what may be called an aesthetic experience. Examining this, first of all, requires that attention be fixed upon a group or complex of mixed components - varied but combined - which can be found to have variety. Attention is focussed. Secondly, the experience will be found to have some kind of intensity. That is, it can be distinguished and said to exist with novelty or vividness. In the third place, the act can be said to be complete in itself or the experience is recognized as having wholeness or unity, it hangs together as something that can be remembered. (Beardsley, 1958). Without determining the magnitude of this reaction to landscape, we can re-interpret these responses so as to identify aesthetic criteria.

These criteria are variety, vividness, and unity. Each is complex in itself and there is the further complication that they all must exist together. Any composition identified as having aesthetic merit must represent some combination of the three. (Pepper, 1937);

Beardsley, 1958). For emphasis in the following discussion, the order given for the criteria is (1) Unity, (2) Variety, and (3) Vividness.

Aesthetic Criteria

Unity is that concern and expression whereby parts are joined together into a coherent and single harmonious unit. As suggested by the Gestalt psychologists (Koffka, 1935), this quality of wholeness is more than the sum of the parts and is recognized as having an identity of its own. Another way of explaining this is through recognition of dominance and subordinance of parts. Should all pieces of a collection be of apparently equal size, though unusual in the landscape, competition and disunity are likely. Where some one part is larger or more conspicuous, its dominance can be the rallying point about which a total composition is made.

Unity of Water

Water can be examined as a powerful medium in the production of unity. It is the ecological unity about a stream course or body (Craighead and Craighead, 1962). There is the unity of movement, and there is the unity of continuity (Hubbard and Kimball, 1917). The fact of water being a single material that is liquid and seen in opposition to a solid unifies it. It is made cohesive by the presentation of a color or closely associated colors. Its surface configuration, whether linear or expansive within a basin gives cohesion. There is the way in which it reflects light as different from the reflection of light from land and plants about it. (See Fig. 39). Streams and lake bodies have exerted their influence upon the land that contains them. It rests at the bottom of a basin or of a landform corridor. It is the central plane of a lake surface.

Fig. 42 - Light reflection off water, distinction
and source of unity

With water as the most active agent in the production of landform, there is the visual stability to be expected between the fit of land and water. In the youthful stream, exuberant and varied in its move-ment, there is the potential misfit relationship to landscape where the two may not yet demonstrate unity together. But there is the continuity of the water as a single kind of material and it maintains its own identity. The young stream exemplifies the way in which the criterion of unity overlaps with that of variety.

Fragmentation of parts or mere repetition of similar parts suggest negative distractions that are apart from unity. Land masses or plants are more prone to demonstrate fragmentation or tedious repetition than may water. Disruptions in the unifying characteristics of water can be expected to be man-made rather than natural. For all its contributions to aesthetic quality, water in its basic unification, its capacity to provide connection in the landscape should be recognized as its one most significant visual role.

Variety

Variety is the second standard for recognizing the presence of aesthetic quality. Richness or diversity are other ways of naming the same characteristic. Interestingly enough, diversity is as much a concern to ecology as it is to aesthetic quality. (Dasmann, 1968). The development of an index to variety (or a density scale for richness) suggests a procedure by which this characteristic can be documented. Variety does have a potential conflict with unity. But this is a paradox as Pepper indicates - a conflict of apparently hostile elements being found together and yet contributing to quality (Pepper, 1937). Richness does not merely suggest the need of many different and diverse parts but implies that they must enjoy organization. From the standpoint of the observer - or more accurately a number of observers with different objectives - the presence of variety insures a maximum opportunity for visual stimulus to all.

Water in the landscape can be examined for a number of ways in which it expresses variety. Water movement (while in general a kind of unification also) demonstrates or can demonstrate variety all the way from slack water with no apparent movement to the dominant and turbulent action of chutes and waterfalls. All degrees of movement between these two extremes can lie within the bounds of a single stream. With movement there is coupled the plane of the surface which may be vertical, in the case of falls, followed by all angular stages down to the flatness of pools where the water is seen as horizontal. With the degree of action there is the connected relationship to color and surface texture running from lightness and roughness to darkness and smoothness. On lakes of irregular outline, a small sheltered embayment can be expected to show a placid surface while its larger connective parent body may reflect the action of wind driven waves. Stream course alignments will be found showing variety in different reaches from meanders to straight stretches – with all stages between the two and in various relationships to one another.

Combinations between water and land demonstrate another kind of linked variety. The narrow and dashing stream may often be accompanied by the tight enclosure of steep land faces; broad and smooth water segments can be expected in horizontal land enclosure with a sense of mutually quiet attitude. Narrow water bodies may carry with them a complete canopy of trees, showing darkness of low level light and separation from the sky. Wide and open expanses suggest highlight

intensity, the relegation of plants to distant edges, and perhaps
the reflection of clouds upon the water surface. Changes in the
orientation of a stream course or an elongated lake carry with them
particular kinds of adjustment to land mass and to plants. A change
of alignment may be accompanied by the exposure of some particularly
distinct cliff or hard rock feature marking the bend. East-West alignment indicates the potential of maximum difference between north-
facing and south-facing slopes. This is a condition most apt to be
accompanied by changes of contrasting kinds of plants, each in its
own microclimate. By comparison, north-south alignment more nearly
implies similar plant relationships for either side of the stream
corridor.

The existence of tremendous diversity found within the pervasive
unity of river systems has been identified by Leopold. In design
terms there are several integrative themes which can tie diversity
and unit together. These are: repetition, segregation, and gradation.
(Pepper, 1937; Simonds, 1961). Repetition is so commonplace in the
landscape that it may attract little or no notice, then perhaps only
as monotony is produced. Yet, for example, a young stream may often
combine a series of meander sets separated by short stretches of
fast white water. The meanders may typically be accompanied by a
willow flat, the fast water by spruce patches. Segregation is a
somewhat more complex kind of repetition, involving more and different
kinds of elements being repeated in random or rhythmic order.

For example, sage slope and dense fir forest, laminar flow and white water rapids, hardrock palisades and gravel outwash plains could all be brought together in various combinations. Recognition of segregation may involve an extensive set of visual sequences seen over an extended period of time. Gradation is that ordered variety which ends in a climax or which builds toward a climax. While segregation is apt to be involved, gradation as a linear process is implied for either a stream or a lake. Using a lake as an example, the outfall area could consist of a broad, flattened landscape with slow water moving out through reeds. Midway to the inlet a series of steepening noses, rocky, with stringers of conifers approaching the water, would present more points of interest and increasing enclosure. The lake head might consist of a hanging valley, with sheer rock face, the inlet stream being a waterfall feature with a sheer drop into deep water. Gradation of the three, most clearly indicates aesthetic quality. It produces vividness.

The assembly of more and varied elements, particularly as they may be seen in orderly fashion helps to identify quality. The different ways in which different components are brought together also indicates an overlap with the criterion of vividness. Finally, it is worth observing that man-made impacts tend to move in the direction of eliminating variety, suggesting a fundamental way whereby degradation by modification may occur.

Vividness

Vividness in the landscape, and especially as found in water
expression, is that quality which gives distinction or produces a
strong visual impression. It can apply to a single composition or
to a series of compositions seen over time. Making use of variety,
vividness grows out of the combining together of different things.
Note how the means of ordering variety combine with the criterion of
vividness.

Contrast, the placing together of dissimilarities, is the primary
way of giving distinction. A more subtle kind of vividness comes out
of mutual accentuation as similar but somewhat differing parts reinforcing one another. Between contrast and similarities there is the
somewhat hazy middleground which Beardsley calls, "indifferent
differences." If contrast is sharp and clear, demonstrating high
quality, then indifferent differences represents indistinction and
mediocrity. However, in the sense that the landscape is large and
seen only over a period of extended time, indifferent difference serves
the important function of providing a simple, undemanding impression
that may be compared against a vivid one.

Returning to water as a source of vividness, many examples have
been given in the classification discussion. The lower and quiet end
of a plunge pool is a maximum contrast for adjacent waterfall - their
principal line attitudes are opposite as are their surfaces and colors.
Immediate changes from fast water to quiet are vivid; gradual transition

from fast water to slow lacks distinction. (Dearinger, 1968). Vividness demonstrated through the device of similarity can be suggested
by an example of broken and turbulent white water accompanied by enclosure of irregular rocky faces along with individual trees of different
ages or with separated clumps of trees and plants together.

The presence of vividness may often indicate the presence of
features, whether those of water, landform or trees. Perhaps some
combination of all may be involved. With distinction there is the
good likelihood of a placename being given: "Deadman's Pool", "Han-
cock Grove", or "Bare Bluff".

Because vividness is nothing if not positive it should be the
easiest of qualities to recognize in the landscape. Yet there is the
matter of degree or magnitude which involves discrimination in judgment
and measurement in relation to regional characteristics. Man-made
modifications can also produce vividness, either through contrasts or
similarities in executed changes. Satisfactory results can only be
expected through careful appraisal followed by good planning and design;
results stemming from mere chance or the application of expediency can
be expected to fail.

Application of the three criteria should be thought of as a process
of integration and synthesis. In the identification of quality no
single criterion is adequate by itself and the three together can be
expected to vary in their proportional weight. Together they represent

a continuum, just as do the items of classification and inventory to
which they apply. It might seem to be an attractive simplification
to link an arbitrary number system with each of the criteria, such as
a ranking from one to ten. But there remains the dilemma that each
individual measure might logically carry a different weight under
different cirucmstances. An arbitrary number assigned necessarily
represents some individual's judgment, and it might appear to be a
statistical fact that could be quite misleading. The use of a nu-
merical system at this time can only be recommended as a convenient
summary if it also relates to a careful and thorough descriptive
analysis.

Empirical data, based upon dependable environmental dimensions
(Craik, 1968) are much needed to assist those who have the responsibility
in making landscape - waterscape evaluations. But aesthetic criteria
are not whimsical nor are they spur of the moment ideas. They are not
determined by popularity contests. They represent a body of knowledge
and need to be applied by those who are competent in their application.

High-Low Quality Comparison

The preceding discussion of aesthetic criteria as well as that
within the classification section serve as an introduction to the
quality comparison listings which follow. Using the basic classification units; landscape unit, setting unit, and waterscape unit,
selected examples of high and low quality are brought together for
comparison. While these listings cannot be exhaustive, they suggest

a wide range of considerations and relationships. Their purpose is
also to suggest other possibilities that will occur to those who
examine the list and have cause for making specific applications. It
is the intention that the examples be reasonably concrete and tangible
representations of the more elusive general criteria of unity, variety,
and vividness.

Classification Framework:

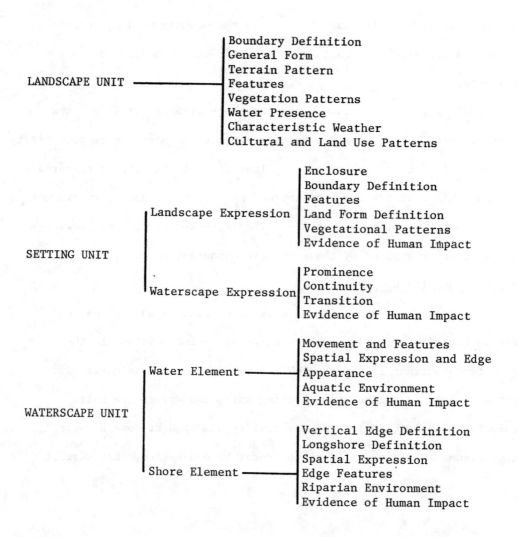

LANDSCAPE UNIT
- Boundary Definition
- General Form
- Terrain Pattern
- Features
- Vegetation Patterns
- Water Presence
- Characteristic Weather
- Cultural and Land Use Patterns

SETTING UNIT

Landscape Expression
- Enclosure
- Boundary Definition
- Features
- Land Form Definition
- Vegetational Patterns
- Evidence of Human Impact

Waterscape Expression
- Prominence
- Continuity
- Transition
- Evidence of Human Impact

WATERSCAPE UNIT

Water Element
- Movement and Features
- Spatial Expression and Edge
- Appearance
- Aquatic Environment
- Evidence of Human Impact

Shore Element
- Vertical Edge Definition
- Longshore Definition
- Spatial Expression
- Edge Features
- Riparian Environment
- Evidence of Human Impact

Listing of Comparative Aesthetic Quality for the Components of the
Classification Framework

LANDSCAPE UNIT _____

Boundary Definition _____

Aesthetic Criteria	Description of Higher Quality	Description of Lower Quality
Unity	Strongly apparent edge surrounds the regional landscape unit. Consistent break contrast from surrounding landscape units. The Sierra and Coastal Range foothills defining the Central Valley. Boundary is always apparent as one enters or leaves the landscape unit. Large islands.	Vague definition of edge or sections of boundary where edge not apparent. Portions of boundary where edge sharply defined contrast with vague or absent edges. Boundary is not usually apparent as one is entering or leaving the landscape unit.
Variety	Variation in edge definition on landscape unit sides are an orienting force to observer. Apparent which side of unit one is passing through- as grassland foothills to mountain unit to open desert.	Variation in edge definition without consistency to a side or sides of the landscape. Variation both tends to confuse orientation within the unit and blur the edges with external units.
Vividness	Contrast between adjacent landscape units produces striking edge definition. Sierra Nevada escarpment to the Owens Valley. Water border - Isle Royale.	Contrast formed by juxtaposition of undisturbed natural and disturbed unnatural conditions, as the Tillamook burn scar to surrounding forest.

General Form _____

Unity	Strongly apparent internal consistency developed by repetition of forms. The internal consistency of forms contrasts with evidently different forms outside the unit. Forms exist within unit and do not repeat outside unit. Undulating cluster of hills surrounded by a vast flat prairie.	Land forms do not consistently exist within landscape unit and are characteristic of surrounding landscape units. Land forms transcend the boundaries of the landscape unit. No consistent pattern developed from land forms that would strongly characterize unit.

LANDSCAPE UNIT - continued

Variety   Combination of adjoining   Landform so repeated and
          and/or opposing land forms   common to region that it
          develops dramatic patterns   tends to monotony. Flat
          and contrasts. Razor-back   plains in west Texas, low
          ridges alternating with flood   very slightly rolling hills
          plain valleys as Appalachians   on the American prairie.
          of western Pennsylvania.

Vividness Presence of single landform   No sharp or abrupt breaks to
          or combination of landforms   contours, all transitions
          unique in comparison to   between landforms gentle and
          all surrounding landscape   gradual. Sharp contrast
          units, the region, and pos-   formed by juxtaposition of
          sibly the entire country.   undisturbed and disturbed
          Yosemite Valley, the Bad-   landforms. Strip mining
          lands of Dakota.   gouges and tailings, eroded
                                            hillsides and gully formation
                                            in Appalachia.

Terrain Pattern

Unity   Particular terrain pattern   No single terrain pattern
          strongly characterizes the   dominates or characterizes
          landscape unit and disting-   the landscape unit. Terrain
          uishes it from surrounding   pattern extends beyond unit,
          landscape units. Broad   common to larger region.
          flood plain of Missouri River,
          the Black Hills of Dakota.

          Terrain pattern consistently   The appearance of water
          associated with presence of a   is evidently incidental to
          water pattern. Trellis drainage the combination of land
          in folded terrain in western   forms. Reservoirs in desert
          Pennsylvania.   conditions.

Vividness Pattern developed by terrain in Pattern developed by terrain
          landscape unit contrasts with   vaguely apparent or not at
          the larger region. Unique   all evident. Landscape unit
          to wide geographic area, pos-   appears to consist of randomly
          sibly unique to country.   associated landforms - no
          Grand Canyon, Monument Valley.   consistent repetitions or over-
          Landforms composing pattern   all compositional relationship
          in high relief, composed of   among landforms. Low,
          highly dissected topography.   inconspicuous landforms com-
          Vivid landforms such as buttes,   pose terrain pattern.
          pinnacles, canyons, steep
          slopes - compose the terrain
          patterns.

LANDSCAPE UNIT - continued

Vividness   Strong contrast developed   Vivid contrasts developed by
            by dominant and sub-dominant   undisturbed natural condi-
            cover. Water presence de-   tions adjacent to disturbed
            fined by vegetational   conditions. Water presence
            contrasts. Vegetation type   obscured by vegetation - no
            evidently associated with   riparian contrast. Vegetation-
            particular land form and   al pattern not strongly re-
            mutually reinforce each   lated to land form types.
            others presence.   Sage cover on slopes and
                                               valley floor.

Water Presence

Unity   Water evidently continuous   Water inconspicuous in unit
            throughout unit - of a size   due to climate or vegetational
            or uniformity of expression   obscuration. Water appears
            to link surrounding land   as isolated bodies throughout
            area into a regional unity.   unit - no evident drainage
            Great Salt Lake, Lake Tahoe,   connection. Apparently random
            Mississippi Delta. Type of   scattering of small water
            water expression unique or   bodies throughout unit. Type
            characteristic to unit and   of water expression not
            does not extend to surround-   characteristic of unit and
            ing units.   extends outside boundaries.

Variety   Water presence a rich combina-   Water presence all of a uniform
            tion of flow, size, and ap-   expression without any apparent
            pearance differences. Unit   contrasts from variation. All
            contains, wild raging rivers,   streams impounded into reser-
            placid streams, large lakes,   voirs. Potholes of the prairie
            and small ponds.   arroyos and washes of the desert.

Vividness   Water rare for region and only   Relatively common and not strik-
            exists within particular land-   ing. So ubiquitous in region
            scape unit. Water has unique   as to be more apparent than land.
            characteristic in comparison   Everglades, Mississippi and
            to the larger region, state,   Sacramento Deltas.
            country.

Characteristic Weather

Unity   Climate localized for the par-   Climate not localized to the
            ticular unit. Strongly con-   landscape unit - no distinction
            trasts with climate outside   of weather is apparent to the
            the region. Death Valley,   unit that does not exist in the
            rain forests of Olympic   surrounding region.
            Peninsula.

LANDSCAPE UNIT - continued

Variety	Contrast in climate offers year round attractions. Changing appearance of land and water. Spring flow of waterfalls, ice cover of lakes, snow patterns on stone cliffs, spring or fall vegetation color.	Climate constant without a change. Constantly hostile conditions - excessive heat, rain, wind, fog, dust and sand storms. Extreme changes in precipitation produce flood and drought conditions in water courses - extreme fluctuation of water level.
Vividness	Clear sky and strong sunlight sharply define landscape forms and features, cast brilliant reflections off water bodies. Ridgelines and peaks etched against the sky. Temperature contrast strongly developed between coolness of water and heat - aridity of surrounding landscape.	Weather such as low clouds, rain, fog usually obscures the surrounding landscape. No temperature contrast between water and surrounding land. Water in a cool, wet climate.

Cultural and Land Use Patterns

Unity	Consistent pattern within landscape unit that does not extend to larger region. Valley in crop pattern surrounded by continuous forest cover. Development patterns reinforce natural patterns. Highways paralleling drainage courses, fences following contour lines.	Development has no apparent pattern and appears to sprawl across the landscape. Development forms no apparent pattern or the pattern that is evident conflicts with the natural pattern. Highways zigzaging across drainage pattern.
Variety	Increase the richness of variation in natural patterns. Planting of hedgerows and field borders on flat plains; breaking of continuous forest cover with openings of meadows.	Development has evidently decreased the natural diversity by imposing a structured pattern of conformity. Grid street and utility layout. Removal of indigenous vegetation.
Vividness	Development of striking features. Country estates along the rivers of tidewater Virginia and Maryland. Provide strong contrast to natural sweep of the land or water. Town cluster.	Development of features that degrade the surrounding landscape. Industrial operations. mining scars, dumps, production of smoke and particulate matter, utility grids, billboards.

LANDSCAPE UNIT - continued

Features

Unity   Features have evident inter-   Interrelationship not evi-
          relationship, same material,   dent among features.
          form, color texture. Ar-   Features appear to be ran-
          ranged in compositional   domly scattered about the
          groups to form pattern.   landscape unit.
          A chain of lakes, a ridge de-
          fined by a row of outcropings.

Variety   Presence of many distinctly   Decreasing conspicuousness
          different features within   of feature by consistent rep-
          landscape unit. Exceptional   etition of single feature
          richness of feature content-   throughout landscape unit.
          Yellowstone Park.   Potholes on Dakota prarie.
          Contrasting of two features
          by juxtaposition- cliff into
          pond, pinnacle rising from
          meadow plain.

Vividness Presence of exceptionally   Features are small in scale
          large features- highest wa-   and common throughout region-
          terfall, pinnacle, peak in   not specific to landscape
          region, state or perhaps,   unit.
          country.
          Feature of such unique dis
          tinction that it identifies
          landscape unit. Niagra-
          Horseshoe Falls, Devils Tower,
          Giant Sequoias.

Vegetational Patterns

Unity   Entire landscape unit cover-   No consistent vegetational
          ed by one consistent vegeta-   pattern characterizes the
          tional pattern that is dis-   landscape unit. Mixture of
          tinctive to the unit and does   several vegpatterns that ex-
          not extend beyond the unit.   tend outside of the unit.
          Great Dismal Swamp, Napa   Chaotic mixture of many veg-
          Valley vineyards.   etational communities do not
                                                combine to form a comprehend-
                                                able pattern.

Variety   Many seperately identifiable   Uniform cover with break in
          vegetation types form a rich   expressiom. All one vegeta-
          pattern composition.   tion type or appearance- as
          Consistently expressed con   all spruce or fir, all tundra,
          trasts among a variety of   over entire region.
          adjoining-opposing vegeta-
          tional zones. Bald grassy
          ridges, conifer slopes, ri-
          parian drainage courses.

SETTING UNIT

Landscape Expression - Enclosure

Unity — Evident spatial dimension and limits to setting. Space enclosed by setting appears to be measurable with no vague openings into other settings. Crater or caldera definition.

Setting configuration produces vague and detached extensions of space. Total enclosure of setting never apparent from any vantage point. Limits to enclosure weakly defined-space of one setting drifts into spaces of adjoining settings.

Variety — Contrast of scales within enclosure - small scale side enclosures into large scale central enclosure.

Uniform scale within total enclosure. Variations inconspicuous.

Contrast between types and degree of enclosure - transition from completely open to strongly enclosed symmetric corridor.

Continuous type and degree of enclosure all along route.

Vividness — Ratio of depth over width highest in region.

Ratio of depth to width average to region.

Average elevational difference between height of enclosure rim and water body greatest in region.

Depth average to region - width of setting greater than average.

Area - width - length - depth, etc. or great or unique for region.

Common to region - average dimensions.

Panoramic - many distant focal points.

Oppressively confining-bottom of trench. Claustrophic condition.

Landscape Expression - Boundary Definition

Unity — Recognizable edge to enclosure. Setting rim strongly defined. Regular basin, symmetric corridor with focal feature closures.

Vague definition - neither feeling of enclosure or openess. Ill defined edges Continual absence of enclosure - agoraphobic condition.

SETTING UNIT- continued

Variety	Adjacent and opposing land-forms create dramatic contrast. Gradual slope to vertical out-crops, pinnacles or cliffs. Flat flood plain opposite river cut bluff.	Adjacent and opposing landforms indifferently different. Neither evident expression of continuity or contrast.
	Contrast in sequential land-forms along water course. Can-yon walls opening to flood plain. Flood plain con-stricting to young, eroding valley.	Monotonous repetition of landform along water course - continuous flat plains and low hills, continuous conifer covered, uniform slope.
Vividness	Uniqueness of landform to region. Widest flood plain, longest and highest continuous escarpment. Highly dissected hill and valley relief. Bold shoulders cut by deep ravines.	Common to region. In-conspicuous because of ubiquity. Conspicuousness due to disturbed condition, ero-sional topography from logging, grading cut and fill faces.

Landscape Expression - Vegetation Patterns

Unity	Entire setting covered by single vegetation type. Con-sistent symmetry of vegetation-al zones up opposing valley slopes.	No vegetation pattern apparent. Chaotic mixture of many assorted vegetation types.
	Strongly defined pattern con-forms to setting - contributes internal consistency. Set-ting characterized by domin-ant conifer cover within and grassland externally dominant.	Vegetation density and height obscures water presence, landform definition, and features. Severely limits the number of vantage points within setting.
Variety	Strongly developed pattern from consistent variety with-in setting. Contrast between north and south facing slopes, riparian and non-riparian, and high elevations and lower elevations. Bald ridges and forested slopes. Pattern developed within setting con-trasts with adjacent setting vegetational pattern.	Vegetation pattern weakly defined. Neither consistent cover or contrasting ex-pression. Apparently ran-dom distribution of vegeta-tional types. Variety in-creased to chaotic degree by introduction of exotic species in unrelated plant-ings. Variety decreased by forest practices.

SETTING UNIT - continued

| Vividness | Sharply defined edges. Prominent ridges against the sky or outlined against distant horizons. Edge itself stands out from setting—bald ridge to forested slopes, rock outcrops to grassland slopes. | Vague edges that blend with setting and external settings beyond. Ridge line difficult to distinguish. |

Landscape Expression - Features

Unity	Features have evident interrelationship, same material, color, and texture. Arranged in compositional groups to form pattern.	Interrelationship not evident among features, chaotic assemblage. Appear to be scattered randomly about setting.
Vividness	Presence of large features – highest peak in region, largest or tallest escarpment. Regionally distinctive or conspicuous.	No distinctive features. Numerous small features with a common appearance.
	Feature present as backdrop to body of water - reflected image in water.	Feature not visibly related to water presence.
	Feature coincides and reinforces focal direction of water - feature at corridor enclosure termination.	Feature in a position to water body so as not to be visible along or across water surface.
	Water feature apparent within setting.	Water feature hidden by vegetation/terrains - hazardous access.

Landscape Expression - Land Form Definition

| Unity | Consistent pattern evident around setting. Entire setting composed of consistent land form expression. Slope definition of undulating hill and swale repetition. Encircling scree slope. Opposing canyon walls. | Inconsistent and varying combination of land forms without evident pattern. Opposing slopes of valley unrelated. |

SETTING UNIT - continued

| Vividness | Striking contrast between adjacent settings. Shady moist riparian forest to open flats of meadow and sage. | Contrast between natural and disturbed vegetation patterns - clear cut balds, fire scars, earth and snowslides adjoining virgin stands. |
| | Unique vegetation cover associated with setting, as tallest redwoods, most extensive flat of cottonwoods, alder, or aspen. | Vegetation cover extends homogeniously over entire region without exception to any setting. Tiaga cover in south central Alaska, fir forests of Oregon. Wheatlands of prairie. |

Water	Expression - Prominence	
Unity	Size and appearance of water body and the enclosing setting harmoniously balance one another. Unifying proportions.	Size and appearance of water body out of scale with setting that encloses it. Water body oversized or undersized to setting, as misfit river, or reservoir/drowned valley.
Variety	Contrasts in prominence of waterscape within setting unit. Narrow stream widens into lake, lake changes to wide stream meanders.	Constant size and appearance of waterscape through setting unit - no variation apparent.
	Contrasts in degree of water prominence in sequence of vantage points around the setting. Surprising changes of water image.	Prominence of water unchanged from all vantage points in the setting. Image of size and appearance remain constant.
Vividness	Evident movement features as rapids, waterfalls.	Still water - no movement evident.
	Large expanse of water surface evident.	Narrow streak of area of surface water insignificant in scale to surrounding setting.
	Striking appearance by virtue of clarity, color or light reflection.	Water appearance backgrounds or blends with setting. Brown-green water color blends with setting. Water usually seen at non-reflective angles.

SETTING UNIT - continued

Water	Expression - Continuity	
Unity	Waterscape has strongly defined internal unity that extends beyond setting (usually in two directions) to imply distant continuity with other settings.	Weakly defined continuity-waterscape composed of segmented reaches or bodies without a well-expressed connective and directive link.
	Changes in setting unit are reflected by a change in the waterscape unit, or a change to a different waterscape unit. Edge of waterscape unit and setting unit coincident.	Changes in setting unit have no apparent relation with the character of the waterscape unit.
Variety	Adjacent waterscape units provide striking contrast within setting unit.	Adjacent waterscape units provide clashing contrast within setting unit - as wild flow into dammed stagnant stretch.
Vividness	Distant views of waterscape beyond either end of setting unit.	Waterscape can not be seen to be totally within or without the setting unit.

Water	Expression - Transition	
Unity	Shore definition acts as transition grade to link water to setting. Dramatic sweep from water to shore to setting in harmonious continuity of transition.	Shore and setting definitions appear unrelated to each other. Neither continuity or contrast expression to their juncture.
Variety	Dramatic alteration between contrast and harmonious blending of shore to setting. Beach to cliff face bounded to beach to low meadow transitions. Break in canyon walls by side valley notches.	Monotonous continuity of same transition expression all along shore and setting juncture. Continuous low mud bank to willow flat transitions along river.
Vividness	Striking contrast between shore definition and setting definition. Gentle broad beach to towering granite cliffs.	Clashing contrast between shore definition and setting definition. Contrast between degraded and pristine, eroding and stable. Recession rim of reservoir adjoining a forested preserve.

WATERSCAPE UNIT _____

Water Element - Movement _____

Vividness	Presence of vivid features – largest waterfall in region. Greatest stretch of rapids in region. Largest waves.	Evidently impounded flow. Imperceptible water movement.
Variety	Rapids alternating with pools Large still pools in otherwise raging river.	Continuous type of movement without contrast. Always wave movement – never placid.
	Conspicuous natural drift material. Leaves, driftwood.	Flood, debris, algae, tires, litter, trash.

Water Element - Spatial Expression _____

Vividness	Largest, widest, longest water surface in region.	Type of water expression common to region, inconspicuous due to ubiquity.
Unity	Waterline consistent with edge definition - little seasonal fluctuation. Stabile in high flow.	Waterline below or above edge definition-flood, low flow. Destructive in high flow.
	Size of water body in fit with setting it has formed.	Water body larger or smaller than setting would naturally indicate.
	Recognizable pattern. Ability to see considerable distances along reaches of water. Focal quality of water path.	Segmented sections without a coherent pattern. Unnatural termination of water along course. Views along water path short and broken.
Variety	Contrast between recognizable patterns. Meanders in an otherwise sinuous river. Changes apparent.	Same – repetitious pattern – all meanders, or sinuous stretches, etc./excessive amounts of sameness.
	Contrast of small spaces to large spaces. Arms, bays, straights contrasted to center of lake. Narrow streams opening up to broad rivers. Wide rivers bifurcating into narrow channels.	All uniformly open, regular unindented shore. Uniform width of water.
	Presence of islands, bars, weathered and water sculptures rocks, boulders.	Unbroken sheet of water. Snags, rocks and bars exposed in low flow or drawdown.

WATERSCAPE UNIT - continued

Water Element - Appearance

Vividness	Color bluest sky blue - bluest in area.	Green, brown.
	Clearest body of water in region.	Water more turbid than most bodies in region.
	Transparent to bottom that has pleasing texture and composition. (Sand and cobbles)	Not transparent because of of turbidity, floating material, etc. Transparent to displeasing bottom condition. (Mud, weeds). Bottom texture and composition unattractive.
Unity	Water body all one color-homogeneous appearance.	Water body has several colors - mottled appearrance. (Salt lakes).
	Water body has even gradation of clarity according to depth. No turbid spots apparent.	Evidently turbid areas of water contrast with clearer depths.
	Mirror-like quality. Ability to reflect setting.	Water always in motion, no reflected images.

Water Element - Aquatic Environment

Variety	Pleasing shore transition patterns. Pleasing colors, textures and contrast to shore definition. (Reeds to cattails).	Proliferation of vegetation to weed level, choke off open water. False shoreline.
Vividness	Pleasing species - frogs, turtles, fish (seen in water or jumping from it), water birds, beavers, etc.	Trash fish. Pests. Annoying insects, snakes, water rats.
	Striking clusters of vegetation in seasonal color or bloom. Flowering water lilies.	Floating mats of weeds. Peat bog condition.

WATERSCAPE UNIT - continued

Shore Element - Vertical Edge Definition
_____

Variety   Dramatic contrast between the   Clashing of natural and
           gradual and abrupt definitions.   unnatural, disturbed and
           Gentle beach to steep rock   undisturbed forms.
           cliff. Riparian skim and
           cliff. Harmonious gradation   No consistent pattern
           of individual forms into a   developed by adjoining
           vertical pattern, as layers   forms.
           of riparian vegetation, sand-
           cobble-boulder. Repetition
           of individual forms into
           pattern.

Vividness Highest cliff in region.   Shore definition so
           Widest beach in region.   common to area as not
                                                to be noticeable.

           Form unique to region. Only   Form common to region
           palisade, only sand beach,   undistinctive due to
           etc.   ubiquity.

           Bold, abrupt rock face.   Evident erosion face-
           Evidently resistent to   disturbed vegetation and
           sheet and/or wave erosion.   gullying scars. Under-
                                                cut and collapsing cliffs.

           Promintory or point defi-   All vertical edge defini-
           nition, edge form thrust   tions on same longshore
           forward from normal shore-   plane.
           line.

           Shore edge stands out in   Shore appears to be un-
           dramatic contrast to   related to water body.
           water.   Water has not formed
           Shore directly related to   shore. Displeasing
           water body.   material. Recession
                                                shore - wide and unin-
                                                teresting. Shoreline
                                                fill.

Unity   Harmonious gradation bet-   Shore edge overgrown by
           ween emerging aquatic veg-   vegetation to obscure
           tation and shore form.   junction definition.

           Apparent balance/harmony   Shore overpowers water
           between water and shore.   expression. Misfit rela-
                                                tionship.

WATERSCAPE UNIT - continued

Shore Element - Longshore Definition
_____

Variety | Repetitious variation discernable in striking patterns. Cut banks and point bars. | Shore definitions chaotic variability. No organizing pattern apparent. Shore definition monotonously constant.

| Opposing shores' variability appears interrelated. (Corridor expression only.) | The variability developed so each shore appears unrelated.

Vividness | Dramatic contrast between adjacent vertical edge definitions. | No contrast evident from a continuous shoretype.

| Dramatic contrast between opposing edge definitions. (Corridor definition only). | Opposing edges clash. Disturbed/unstable/degraded versus stable/natural.

Unity | Opposing edge definitions are symmetrical to unsymmetrical in related pairings. | No relationship apparent between opposing edge definitions. Chaotic arrangement.

| Opposing sides harmoniously balance and complement. (Corridor expression only). Strong visual continuity formed by recurring shore definitions or patterns | Opposing sides clash. Contrast between disturbed and undistrubed shores. Monotonous continuity formed by nonvariable shore definition. No apparent continuity formed by chaotic variation of longshore definitions.

Shore Element - Spatial Expression
_____

Vividness | Greatest ratio of height to distance between opposing shores in region. Ratio lowest in region. | Average ratio of height to distance between opposing shores in region.

| Average height of shore definition greatest in region. Greatest height or width, or area covered by the particular shore form in the region. | Average height of shore common to region. Common enough not to be noteworthy.

WATERSCAPE UNIT- continued

Shore Element- Edge Features

Vividness	Spectacular natural features such as waterfalls, caves that are unique in presence or scale to the region.	Disturbance or degraded conditions such as burn scars, erosion scars, accumulations of drift debris.
Unity	Features have evident repetition along the water course. Associated with changes in shore definition such as waterfalls at side stream defiles.	Features randomly located- often at confusing juxtaposition with shore definition. Eccentric boulders from valley wall toppled on beach.

Shore Element - Riparian Environment

Vividness	Vegetation stands out as feature from shore definition. Agricultural, horticultural contrasts. Seasonal color or rarely occuring vegetation. Exceptionally tall trees, heritage trees.	Diseased windblown,stunted, burned, or leaning vegetation. Rank, overgrown patches.
	Observable fauna- otters, raccoons, beavers, shorebirds, amphibians.	Pests- rats, snakes, annoying insects.
Unity	Continual stringers of distinctive vegetation appear along length of water course. Cottonwood, aspen, birch stands.	Exotic vegetation plantings at random intervals along water course. No apparent continuity.

SECTION III

A CLASSIFICATION OF THE MAN-MADE ELEMENTS AND IMPROVEMENTS
RELATED TO LANDSCAPE UNITS, SETTING UNITS, AND WATERSCAPE UNITS

Classification of the alterations which men may make to the
environmental landscape is a complex subject. Not only are we
concerned with minor alterations and modifications to natural
elements, but we must consider the effects of engineering, architecture, and landscape architecture. In order to reduce the
complexity, this study groups similar kinds of constructed elements
or improvements into units which have visual significance. The
details of this classification may be seen on the following few
pages. The central thrust is to extract configurations which may
be seen to have relatively simple forms. The forms chosen are
those which are common to most structures, engineering works, or
landscape architectural alterations and improvements.

The primary emphasis is to single out the elements which can
be seen as a reasonably distinct element against a neutral or uniform background. Even this distinction is somewhat relative.
Each observer is attentive to different elements. It is possible
to cartoon the visual process as having two objectives which are
interactive but which yield different results; the things one sees,
and the things one looks for. The distinction is simple to relate
to everyday experience. Each reader will know the process of
trying to pick out special elements from a complex background;

road signs in the city, for example. On the other hand, the easy
relaxed process of visual rumination which we often refer to as
"just looking" and which implies a less purposeful visual rambling,
is by no means a correspondingly simple process to analyze, even
superficially.

Vision is the primary means for collecting information, clues,
and, impressions from the environment. Simple conservation of
energy demands that we focus upon and concentrate our attention
upon a relatively few elements, searching for the clues we need,
for those which we find pleasurable, and for those which are so
visually prominent that they are difficult to ignore.

Much of the open landscape visible in the Landscape Setting
Unit will be relatively neutral; part of the general terrain, background or cover. A vast and continuous forest is a bland and
neutral visual field, an expanse of extended water landscapes is
similar. Both require intellectual input from the observer if he
is to "see" that which is concealed by the uniformity. In such
seeing and understanding lies the deepest and most lasting visual
pleasure. It is a reward which follows considerable thought and
effort. It is not a superficial reality.

Those elements which emerge with some clarity to our notice
are those which are contrasted from the uniformity of background
and which are sufficiently vivid to be clear. If such elements
are natural elements, are seen in some profusion, and are not
only visible but physically distinguished from others of a

representative type, then we have the makings of a striking landscape; perhaps a dramatic landscape. Waterfalls, high cliffs,
striking contrasts of light and shade, vivid colors; all are examples of such striking and eyecatching elements. As an aside,
the words "striking" and "eye-catching" are words which, in common
use, suggest the positive, physical attraction and force inherent
in such non-background visual elements.

The classification suggested here takes relatively simple,
identifiable elements which are easily seen, names them, and provides a simple framework so that each element may be considered
as it applies to the three land-water configurations classified
elsewhere in this report: landscape units, setting units, and
waterscape units.

MAN-MADE STRUCTURES OR ALTERATIONS IN THE LANDSCAPE UNIT

THE LANDSCAPE UNIT: Linear Elements

The Landscape Unit is primarily defined by its coherance at the large scale. Boundaries are visible or implicitly defined and the details of its extent are sufficiently simple so that there is an overall sense of completeness and entity.

Water at this scale is often seen as a distinct linear element related to its geological setting. Lake shorelines, for example are linear clues to lake form, shoreline, and the landscape container. Shallow water near the shore may be seen as a linear clue to water clarity, bottom character and material, and an indicator of wave action. Meanders are linear at this scale forming patterns which give interest, life, and vitality to the scene.

Linear elements may be perceptible in ways which are significant to the realization of the extent and the boundaries of the Landscape Unit. Some may subdivide the unit into smaller portions of field, forest, and water; some may assist in giving character and expression to the landform, to suggest special boundaries, or to denote the presence of certain materials.

Linear elements such as the profile of a range of mountains can signify a great deal. Not only is there a frame of reference and boundary; it provides, because of its form characteristics, clues to the quality of that boundary. Placid and gentle outlines of geologically old mountains are in vivid contrast to the angularity and ragged quality of younger and more exciting ranges.

Overlapping lines of foreground ridges, gorges, or peaks form a
pattern of significant meaning; a prime source of visual clues
to distance, spatial distribution, and terrain character. Linear
highway or railroad elements may be of sufficient importance to
act as boundaries as may the visible evidence of their construction; cuts, filled areas, clearings or bridges. Other bounding
elements in the linear form are to be seen in the horizons of
large water bodies or banks of fog, cloud, or haze which are
characteristic of their horizons.

The edge of a stand of timber may have a distinct linear form, a common case with windbreak plantings or hydrophytic plants seen growing along a distant streamcourse. These elements assume a linear form because of the coherance and character of the elements themselves. Alternatively, the linear quality may appear as the result of differing contrast or color. Both are important and common forms. Such boundary plantations or clearings often provide the most striking contrasts in landscapes which may be essentially flat and featureless or which may be covered by a uniform growth of forest.

Fig. 43. - Linear plantation of trees along a stream.

Fig. 44 - Linear cut forest boundary.

Linear cut forest margins are rarely enhancing to the landscape except in the limited sense of helping to clarify and delineate
the landform. Most often the extreme contrast which results will
establish a new character for the landscape which is destructive
of natural values. These striking marks of human use engage the
visual attention and establish a special appearance. Preserving
the best natural visual quality in landscape is very difficult when
such elements are visible.

Man-made elements which are not intended to be boundaries are represented by such examples as power lines, canals, water conduit clearings, and highway alignments. These often present extreme contrasts and are, as a result, highly visible. Such structures are visually strong enough to form subdivisions or boundaries in the landscape unit which deflect attention and interest from the most striking or pleasant landscapes.

Fig. 45 - Linear clearings for pipeline.

Natural water boundaries are often modified or altered to solve drainage or flood problems, to provide protection to farm or urban lands or to create more navigable waters. Dikes, levees, and riprap margins are examples of water edge construction which is usually highly linear in form and expression. The natural and character-istic form of the stream bank has been sacrificed in order to deflect the course of the stream, to offer protection to a fragile bank, or to avoid the erosive effect of high water velocities. Man's impact on the land and the superimposition of functional structures has replaced the visible and expressive results of natural form.

Because of the argument for reasonable cost and structural homogeniety, water bounding elements are usually highly uniform in design or cross-section. Because of this unnatural uniformity, they interrupt the continuity of relationship which exists between landscape and water element.

Fig. 46 - Linear water protection forms a barrier to visual access.

There is little to commend solutions which ignore every consideration except cost and efficiency. Parallel dikes which stretch for miles, offer small visual compensation for their economy.

Degraded landscape and the destruction of water's evolutionary
traces is the result of such single-purpose "improvements."

At the scale of the Landscape Unit, linear elements are often
not precisely identifiable. They appear as abstract lines. The
edge of a forest is too far away to judge the tree species; only
the linear edge appears. The river edge is too remote to determine
whether the linear form is natural or flows in a dredged channel.
A railroad and highway form superficially similar linear patterns.
Only the careful or practiced eye will notice the easier curvatures
and the gentler gradients of the rail line.

Man-made linear forms can be made to conform to more humanistic
visual standards and to provide a good setting for reasonable
multiplicity of use. River flood control measures, for example,
need not exclude all considerations except hydraulic efficiency.
Dike alignments and form could vary in appropriate locations, to
accomodate access and recreational use.

Fig. 47 - Recreation and water access within controlled waterway.

Plan and Profile Views

Linear elements appear in two basic forms; those seen mostly
in plan   and those seen mostly in profile. There is rarely a
purity about such separation. Most elements have both profile
and planimetric aspects. Visually, most observers are able to
resolve the complexity in these situations. For example, a line
of towers which traverses a succession of hills may present a
complex visual image from most viewpoints. Even so, as in the
sketch example, it would be obvious to most observers that the
planimetric aspect is a straight line.

If what we see is reasonably close to what we expect, there
is no tendency to look for additional clues. Normally, we expect
the world to be visually clear and simple and act on that assumption.
The probability of simple organization is one of the commonest of
these assumptions and a good thing, too. Design is most strongly
expressed when its forms are straightforward and simple. However,
problems arise when the visual expression for one element is at
visual odds with a different element. Power lines make a distinct
visual interruption in natural landscape because the structure of
wire and towers is unique and distinct relative to the landscape.

This leads to a dilemma in the form of a question which must
be dealt with in any high quality natural landscape where man-made
improvements are present. Can any such designed reorganization or
development set in a strongly formed landscape be enhancing in the
visual sense? The answer is a qualified answer but is, probably
not. The contrasts which are set up in such relationships are at

least partly disruptive of the quality and serenity of that landscape.
What can be done?

There are two possible answers which invite further consideration.
The first is that we must learn to respect the vital nature of our
country's landscapes as a foil to the mechanistic world we are com-
mitted to. Parts of this landscape are too good to spoil; too
visually and environmentally potent to be emasculated by pressing
single-purpose demands. We must learn to identify those areas which
must be preserved and those which warrant conservation, from those
which will need to be altered to accommodate a growing population and
growing industrial, and service requirements. Within these areas
designated for care certain definite visual entities will be seen.
The Landscape Unit is an example. To respect these, we shall have
to find ways to prevent the thoughtless location of visually contrasty and therefore visually disruptive elements. Elements which
can be visually resolved as simple linear forms are very difficult
to conceal or justify. Alternate locations or alternate forms need
to be explored.

A second possible answer, which at first glance may appear to
be an evasion, is that man-made elements can present excellent and
satisfying visual images when the forms adopted are properly limited
to the scale and functional requirements of the problem in question
and when the accommodation of these forms on the land is done with
a minimum of disruption or devastation. Boundaries are critical.
It is here that the contrasts between the forms of modern society

and forms of nature are visually most vivid and where the simpli-
cities of organization conflict with the complexities and the
highly interrelated ecological fabric of the natural landscape.
Boundaries are very often linear forms simply because it is easiest
to measure and apportion land in that way. We position elements so
that they are aligned with boundaries, roads so that they align
with buildings, and canals so that they align with political juris-
dictions. We control rivers so that they flow parallel to highways.
Some of this accommodation to boundaries is economical or is justi-
fiable functionally. In many examples however, these boundaries
are in visual conflict with the best visual qualities of the landscape and water. If the boundary problem is given thoughful consideration, and the design or organization is reflective of
functional needs, there is every reason to assume that man-made
developments can be as visually compelling as natural land and
waterscapes. The solution lies in the preservation, enhancement,
or management of each, according to its basic needs and the care
with which the interfaces between them can be made less vivid.

Visual persistence of linear elements is a powerful force.
When the linear form is a straight line, its accommodation to the
complexity of landscape is difficult. At the natural-developmental
interface it must be carefully used. When water is a linear boundary
at this interface, it will require thoughtful planning to avoid
making a free and strong landscape element into a minor functional
fragment. The contrast potential is so strong that its degraded

state becomes plainly visible to all.

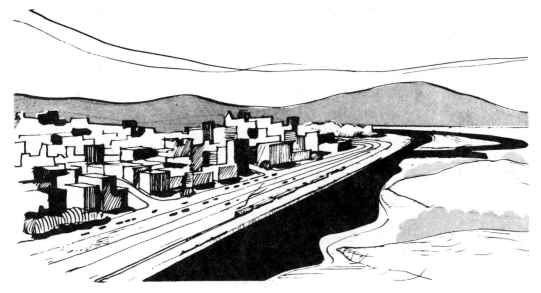

Fig. 48 - Forcing linear configuration on a free-flowing river.
Profile Views

At the scale of the Landscape Unit, linear elements in
profile can be important visual indicators. The outline of distant
mountains may have the exciting angularity of precipitous walls and
gorges, barren rocky faces or scree slopes. That profile may indicate the smoothly rounded and polished faces of glaciated granite.
It may reveal the gentler, softer profile of the older ranges and
the more gentle visual accents which are characteristic of such
mountains.

The profile of stream courses, perceptible at this scale can
reveal much of the character of the stream and of the details of
the landscape over which it flows. Quiet pools or white water
traces are clues to the landscape which we seek to understand.

The presence of white water is a strong visual indicator of terrain gradient. The presence of quiet pools or lake surfaces are indicators of level ground. Volume and scale of the watercourse modifies these visual clues. Deep and narrow streams can flow more smoothly at steeper gradients without conspicuous white water than shallow or wider streams.

It is possible to equate many visual hints seen at Landscape Unit scale, so as to reach a composite opinion, a balancing of visual impressions. These clues, when related to profiles, are important modifiers to factual as well as pleasurable knowledge of the landscape we see.

The structures made by man contain many visual clues. As automobile drivers, we become accustomed to the standards employed for highway gradients and their appearance. When we view the linear profile of a distant road over a range of mountains, we are able to associate those familiar gradients with the setting and to draw useful inferences from that association.

Railroad gradients must be made much gentler than those used for highways. Bridges or trestles much be used to span the gorges and tunnels pierce the spurs if the continuity of gradient is to be managed. These highly visible structures are important indicators of terrain and of distant landscape differentiation. A tunnel opening, a bridge, a snowshed are all important engineering elements necessary for the maintenance of gradient, itself a clue

Fig. 49 - Rail structures define terrain features.

to the topography of landscape. Engineering structures are a

necessity in sharp edged or badly broken terrain. In steep but

broader scaled mountains it is often possible, in maintaining a

railroad gradient, to skirt problem areas by going the longer way

around. In plan, the route would follow a winding course rather

than the straight line permitted by engineering works. The dis-

tant view is characteristically different, the meaning is different.

Such profiles can give us much additional information about the

bulk, the rotundity or the scale of mountain settings.

Fig. 50 - Linear railroad gradients provide visual clues to terrain.

Useful as such clues are to the nature of terrain and scale,
it should be clear that road and railroad profiles are sharply
contrasting elements by their nature and tend to interrupt the
flow of landscape. They stand out sharply against their background. They interrupt the eye scan from valley to mountain top.
They break the continuity of forest cover. Such expressions
in common usage as "the uninterrupted sweep of landscape" or
"soaring peaks" are literary terms that describe the visual action
of the observer as much as they apply to the terrain. Each refers
to the implicit desireability of feel-seeing the sweeping scale of
natural elements, and is suggestive of the disruptive contrast of
structure.

A particular problem posed by linear elements seen in profile
is that they can structurally modify natural profiles. Fill
structures which flatten ridge lines are an example; roads which
cut ridges are another. Excavations made to obtain fill or construction materials for dams, road construction or earthwork projects is a third. In each of these examples the visual consequences
are in vivid contrast to the elements of nature. They become a
highly visual element with important effects on the visual quality
of the Landscape Unit. Highly contrasting elements of this type
can only be regarded as degrading if they destroy or materially
detract from the unity and visual consistency of the Unit.

Fig. 51 - Ridge construction alters character of landscape unit profile.

Fig. 52 - Ridge cut detracts from natural values.

Plan Views

    As the scale of the Landscape Unit increases and the position

of the observer is higher in elevation, man-made linear elements

may be more important in their planimetric aspects than in profile.

In such cases, the displacement of elements like roads or rail-

roads reveal the topographic form by the abruptness or directional

changes; easier terrain, by the rotundity or curvature of the

alignment.

Fig. 53 - Landscape unit boundary formed by road seen planimetrically.

Linear elements seen from high observer viewpoints are potent visual modifiers of the Landscape Unit. For canals, dredged channels, dikes, or powerlines, their linear characteristics become important land divisions. Sometimes, a boundary to the Unit itself when there is no conspicuous landscape boundary. Concerned as we are with the ways in which landscape can retain its visual effectiveness, as well as the ways in which necessary improvements or structures may be designed and constructed, we must classify contrasty bordering elements as among the weakest aesthetic solutions to landscape space definition.

150

Fig. 54 - Road as landscape unit division.

<u>THE LANDSCAPE UNIT</u>: <u>Area Elements</u>

Visual elements which are seen to have an appreciable extent
of surface are classified as area elements in this study. This
distinction implies that there must be some termination to the
quality of surface. Edges may be sharp and distinct, or they may
be relatively soft and diffuse but there must be consistency of
surface so that it is coherant and visually unified. A certain
amount of subdivision is possible without destroying the basic form.
Indeed, a lively visual character often results if there is some
differentiation in the nature of the surface. An important requirement is that the area element be simple in form so that it

separates visually from background complexity. Highly articulated area elements with complex boundaries may have a definite boundary and a highly consistent surface but remain largely invisible because of their complex form.

Landscape and water elements which are able to emerge from the complex of color and texture which we see must have the advantage of clarity and visibility. Enterprising Western fertilizer companies have devised a clever outdoor advertisement demonstration. By carefully sifting fertilizing agents in winter, using a giant stencil the name of the company is made to emerge in lush green grass after the first Spring rains. Not a particularly commendable addition to the natural beauty of the spring landscape but a vivid demonstration of the power to command vision which is characteristic of the requirements for area elements listed above.

Light is one of our most important visual concerns. A brightly sunlit exposure will have the maximum range of possible contrasts, from the blackest shadows to the most dazzling highlight. Reflections of light from polished or smooth surfaces will be a maximum, the outline of shadows will be crisp and sharp, and there will be the best exposition of color. The edges of objects will stand out in brilliant contrast to dark backgrounds, minor differentiation of color is perceptible to the eye, water reflects back the images of the sun in a dazzle, and we find pleasure and delight in the richness of impression, and the range of contrasts.

As the sun moves in its daily or seasonal path, there are
changes to the visual quality of what is illuminated. Early and
late hours bring the greater filtration effects of sunlight
through the atmosphere. Colors are diffused and shadows grow
longer. They obscure more of the nature of the surface. Contrast is greatly reduced. Water in the lower depressions is in
comparatively deep shadow. Edges and boundaries are lost in
lengthening shadow, in diminished contrast, or by loss of color
differentiation. It is obvious that if we wish to have a water
or landscape element seen in a clear relationship to its surroundings, it is necessary that the nature of its illumination be
an important consideration in siting and design. We can site
necessary roads, trails, viewpoints, and structures so that the
best qualities of the landscape and the water will be more vividly
seen in the proper light.

LANDSCAPE UNIT: Regular Areas

At the scale of the Landscape Unit only the largest area
elements will be visible. Examples are towns, or town environs,
airfields, large recreation fields, industrial plants and their
storage or assembly areas. Most such elements in the Landscape
Unit will be regular in form. Economical cost and organizational
efficiency and expression require simplicity. The result is a
highly contrasting form in a landscape setting.

When the Landscape Unit contains predominately urban development, industrial development, or combinations, area boundaries
will tend to become more diffuse -- less definite, contrasty, and
perceptible. Complexity of surface is the norm. Highly contrasting
edges are perceptible only at the boundary between natural and
urban landscape. Water in the midst of such areas could be a
visually significant element offering relief and contrast from
the complexity of urban pattern. When the water element is urbanized,
its shores "improved" in conformity with surrounding urban elements
and its visual qualities concealed by shadows, or altered by pollution, it may become invisible. It may be concealed by the sense-
less transformation of its natural form, lost in the complexity of
urban pattern.

Fig. 55 - Watercourse encased in urban concrete

Special Classes of Areas (4)

There are four other special classes of man-made area elements
which are important at the scale of the Landscape Unit. These are
agricultural areas, forest clearings or logging operations, mining
or quarrying, and flooding.

Agricultural areas are the most prevalent of the area element
types in most parts of this country, except perhaps in mountainous
areas. The landscape of the United States seen from the air, has
few locations without agriculture traces. The scale of agricultural operations is large. The pattern of land surveying adopted
in this country tends to give agricultural land simple and regular
shapes. Machine cultivation and harvest demands regularity of
surface; an important visual consideration. The basic requirements for area elements are present: contrast of boundary, consistency of surface, and simplicity of form. Agricultural areas
form a visible and differentiated pattern of area elements over
much of our landscape.

Thrifty agriculture is not unpleasant to look upon.
(Dearinger, 1968). Perhaps that is because we are not far removed in time and culture from a predominately agricultural life.
It may be that the apparent productivity of the earth, visible
through agriculture, is a pleasant confirmation of the presence
of fertility and the renewal of life. Except in the case of concentrated animal husbandry, where the landscape is trampled, or
overgrazed, or simply used as an enclosure, most agriculture is

visually positive rather than negative; in the general sense
enhancing to a greater degree than degrading.

When a variety of crops are cultivated, the resultant pattern
of area elements can be pleasant indeed. Not only is there an
abundance of color differentiation, and a variety of textural
nuances, but there is considerable recognitive possibility which
is pleasurable.

The second most prevalent area element type in the Landscape
Unit is the forest clearing or lumbering operation. Removal of
timber, especially as it is generally practiced in the western
United States, provides the visual requirements previously listed.
Because most of the timber is removed, the ground surface becomes
remarkably consistent in appearance. It is very like the appearance
of the ground after harvesting agricultural crops. In addition to
continuity of ground surface, the boundaries of the cut-over areas
are usually geometric in shape and are distinct and contrasty.

In time, this area type generates a new surface appearance. In
selfseeding or naturally regenerative landscape environments, the
barren character of the surface slowly gives way to a new, living
cover of low plants, berries, small trees and grasses. The scars
and the earth colors are softened, the dust is washed down, and
a measure of apparent regeneration returns. The area, as a visible
element remains clear and vivid however, for a considerable period.

The edges of the harvested crop remain clear and sharp, differentiated from the new cover crop.

Some lumbering, unlike thrifty agriculture, creates a degraded
visual condition for several basic reasons. The scale of change is
the first problem. It is difficult to bring to mind the expression
"careful husbandry" which is commonly used in reference to agricultural landscapes when the visible results of the harvest operation
are so disruptive. Not only does the conventional method used for
taking the crop result in a littered and torn surface, but the side
effects on adjoining landscapes is a secondary problem. Streams are
littered with trash and broken twigs and flow muddy and rampant with
the changes in runoff volume. Soils are displaced and often
stripped by the erosive action of water in temporary roads and skid-
ways, left after harvest. Waste is evident elsewhere; non-crop
trees are often damaged. The visible result is not harvest in the
best sense of the word, but destruction. It is not surprising that
such operations are concealed by tree screens left along highway
corridors.

This visual degradation can be offset in considerable measure
by positive steps. The first is to undertake studies which will
lead to harvest areas of greater visual complexity so that the area
element will be less blatantly obvious. Some work has been undertaken toward this end. A second positive step is to alter
harvesting practices so that visual side effects such as water

discoloration, trash flotation or stream destruction caused by increasing runoff are eliminated or drastically reduced. A third and most important step is to avoid such harvest practices altogether in those Landscape Units which are of primary visual significance. It may be a problem to institute all of these measures everywhere but certainly the Federal Government should promptly alter its present practices and establish new and strict rules which will ensure the continuation of our forests as a vital resource for water, recreation and visual pleasure as well as for timber. It is probable that water and recreation are going to be more important than wood in the forseeable future.

The third area element in the Landscape Unit is the mining, quarrying or strip mining operation. To varying degrees these processes destroy the ground surface. They expose the contrasting subsurface soil or rock. Customarily, the spoil is cast aside. Trees are removed along with all other cover. The vast amounts of loose material creates problems in adjoining streams. Only occassionally is any consideration given to the process of repair or creative restoration. (Aguar, 1970). Portions of the country are scarred seriously and permanently by the devastation.

Studies made of alternative handling of waste so as to reduce devastation pressured by critical reactions to strip mining in the Southeast, taconite, and coal in other parts of the nation. (Zube, 1963). There have been a few isolated instances where

public reaction has prevented such operations. By every criteria, these
degrading area elements must be controlled, operating methods altered, and
new public consciousness aroused. (Johnson & Sand & Gravel Inst., 1966).

The fourth area element is created by flooding. These created
lakes, reservoirs, storage ponds, or controlled streams have one
primary visual advantage, they provide a visible increase in the
amount of water in the landscape. Most of us would be hard put to
deny this increased acreage as an advantage, except in very specific
terms, which are often related to preservation of natural landscape.

One specific objection within the scope of this study relates
to water level, or more precisely, the relationship of water level
to the landscape. Most impoundment proposals have a certain degree
of flexibility in the height of the water. This flexibility can be
obtained by variations in the height of the dam or the pool level.
Alternate sites for the dam structure and pool offer other variants.
At times, subsidiary storage structures, pumps, linked reservoirs,
and system management permit considerable variation in water level
at a specific point so that scenic advantages can be preserved
while providing for a mix of other needs.

Of critical importance is a water level which is believable.
Natural lakes and streams, during their formation, develop a
visually coherent position in the landscape. There is an un-
mistakeable quality of rightness, of a falling together of all
the dependent elements; of the formation of a visual coherance.

This is the primary quality we must learn to identify, to value, and to preserve.

Almost all lakes and watercourses have a distinct shore. Its visual character will be determined by both the nature of the stream course and the terrain through which it flows. These may range from broad and sandy to clean and scoured. In any case the shore is the visual temporal record of the action of water on its landscape container.

Fig. 56 – Shoreline character is individual to every water body.

Natural lakes exhibit, at their margins, a positive relationship with the landscape. There is a clearly visible zone where the action of the water has made its mark on the land. Sometimes the water level fluctuates from a Spring high to a late Summer low.

This rising and falling water prevents the establishment of a full riparian plant population; only the most adaptable can take intermittent immersion. The result is a distinct gradation of the plant community which borders on the water. In some lakes, the margin has been formed by soil and floating organic material, held by surface tension to the bank, or driven there by the wind. In time these materials become waterlogged and sink into the shallows or may be weighted down and forced under by soil washed from the land or by falling leaves. As this organic debris accumulates, it produces its own characteristic form. In still other instances, rain loosened scree from nearby mountainsides rolls into the water or stops at the shore to form still another kind of distinctive margin.

Whatever the particular nature of this naturally formed shoreline, it is visually right and honest. The manner of its formation is visible to the curious observer and the impression of clarity and simplicity which it creates is universally appealing.

When fluctuating artificial water bodies are created, this characteristic quality of shoreline is missing. The controlled rising and falling water levels act through too great a range of elevations to permit any significant water action on a narrow shore zone. The visual effect is that of a sullied water edge which lacks character. It is totally unlike the shoreline of a naturally formed water body. At the scale of the Landscape Unit, this artificially created shore zone is a distinct visual element.

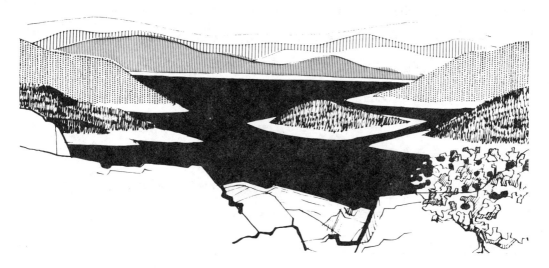

Fig. 57 - Fluctuating reservoir shoreline

In heavy forest, such a shoreline is created by a careful
program of forest harvesting prior to, or during the construction
of a dam. The maximum water level is set out on the ground by
survey teams and the timber harvest follows. Often a special contract for timber in the reservoir is let. The exact specifications
for clearing debris and stump is set forth. The result is variable
but visually predictable. An artifical forest edge is carved out
of the heart of the forest. The protective edge of smaller windbreak and bordering trees is gone. The previously shaded forest
floor is open to the wind and the sun.

When such an edge is newly cut, it is neat and clean. In a
short time, however, the elements act to alter the appearance,
sometimes drastically. At the edge of the cut, wind can cause
considerable casualties to trees which were formerly protected
but which have not developed a sufficiently strong root structure
to resist new wind loads. Exposure of the forest floor to
sunlight stimulates the growth of a new, and visually alien shore
understory huddled under the vertical wall of the cut forest. The
crisp edge becomes ragged and vulnerable. A visual anomaly has
been created in a formerly consistent setting

Fig. 58 - Rank growth occurs at cut edges.

Constructing reservoirs or artificial lakes presents nearly
impossible difficulties with respect to shoreline except in cases

where the reservoir is a structure designed to act as an emergency water source or as a recreation resource. When, as in these examples, the water level can be stabilized, the problem is simpler. It is not necessary to contend with a barren zone, flooded at one season; exposed to the sun in the next.

Some useful time can be spent during reservoir planning, in the identification of terrain segments which may favorably be viewed when they become a shoreline. Rocky outcrops, as an example, form an attractive part of a created shoreline, simply because the need for a shore shelf is not as great. Rocky cliffs, which plunge into the depths with a foreshore are common. Looking at other possibilities, a natural level area or shelf, a ledge or a flat ridge top form an acceptable visual substitute for a naturally created shoreline. Glacial debris or boulders may provide attractive visual incidents.

Grading or reshaping of terrain is perfectly feasible and offers many interesting possibilities. Careful selection of water level with respect to existing plant communities will permit the retention of the most valuable specimens or groups. Some advance clearing at the proposed shoreline may permit the introduction of new plants which can serve as positive visual transition to future water levels, as effective windbreaks, and as shade to prevent rank new understory growth. Such advance planning and cutting, in a relatively narrow corridor may prevent some unattractive and

wasteful tree losses from wind exposure and encourage cover surface
growth which can protect the surface from erosion when the forest
floor is opened to the elements.

A second possibility which is worth careful consideration is
choice of viewpoint. It is possible to select sites which afford
views of the most favorable portions of the reservoir, portions
where the new shoreline is visually consistent with the natural
shoreline or conversely, where the most difficult new shoreline
sections are concealed. Such viewing is commonly centered about
roads and the views afforded from them, at view or rest points,
and at picnic and campground sites. Most visitors do not make a
complete exploration of every scenic or recreation stop they make.
Often, tourists make only superficial contact with major points
of interest on their itinerary. For a large segment of the
traveling public, selection of view opportunities can make a
significant difference. Far too little attention has been paid
to the real possibilities which exist for improving our view of
the natural world and the created elements within it by exclusion
of undesireable prospects. Careful management of position opportunities and the creative development of others can have a
positive beneficial effect.

In the Landscape Unit, the dam itself, despite the scale,
may be a massive element, large enough to be seen as an area element.
In almost all cases, its geometry as well as its distinctive size
or color make it a vivid and compelling, visually dominant element.

In this country, proud as we are of our engineering and construction skills, it is not surprising to find most dams shown off as tourist attractions. Frequently roads and view sites are located, not as a means of gaining a more pleasant and informative view of the countryside, but purely and simply as an advertisement for the strength and awesome majesty of the structure and manifest skill and abilities of the agencies responsible. In case this message has somehow eluded the jaded motorist, large billboards are placed as foreground reminders. Often the viewpoint contains a display of maps, photographs and statistics which glorify the project as well as the agency.

Such displays, such agency pride is not all misplaced. Indeed, information and education is necessary for the traveling public. The emphasis is important, however. These places and their access roads should be moved somewhat out of the public eye so that the visual emphasis is placed on the best values of our national landscape with its water and forest scenic resources.

In the Landscape Unit, it is often possible to site a proposed dam, or alternatively, a road so that the major developed views to the unit will be those which focus attention on the scenic merits of water and landscape. Education displays and access roads to powerhouses can be clearly marked turnoffs from these main roads.

The planimetric aspect of lakes and reservoirs, as well as the large and slower moving fluvial water bodies are of significant visual importance as a reference datum. The leveling of a water

body serves as a valuable reference to the visual "lie" of the
landscape and to the relative steepness of adjacent ground. Other
area elements which are regular in form such as farm fields, urban
street patterns, or clearings may be useful in a similar way. Only
still water, however, is understood to be unfailingly level.

PLANIMETRIC AREA ELEMENTS: Irregular Areas, Planimetric Aspects

Water serves as to define landscape topography. Variance in
topography is revealed by the configuration of the plane of the
water surface. The more complex irregularity, the more complex the
three dimensional aspects of the landform. Water makes the reality
of landscape form visible -- one of its most significant attributes.

The reverse aspect of the question is of vital concern in any
discussion of controlled water level. Because the plane of the
water reveals the shoreline form, that form can be materially
altered by variance in water level.

Some work has been done on reservoir site selection which
evaluates alternative sites in respect to shoreline form. It
would help to know about public reaction to possible forms for
reservoir shoreline so that a positive evaluative tool for
specific design proposals could be developed. In spite of this
lack, it is reasonably certain that more complex shoreline form
is more interesting than that which is perfectly plain and regular.
Complex shore forms are likely to present more interesting view
opportunities, better framing or enclosure for Waterscape Units,

more wind shelter, and certainly a longer shoreline length. Such
length offers more opportunity for immediate water experience,
and better chance to space out, to seclude or conceal, needed development nodes, one from the other.

Fig. 59 - Complex shorelines are scenically interesting.

Proposed water levels may be raised or lowered so that the
configuration of the shoreline is more useful as well as more interesting. Such adjustment can generate usable recreational land
adjacent to the shoreline. Many lakes or reservoirs are single
purpose projects. Some will have little in the way of multiple
uses, being limited to drinking or irrigation water supply. However, most water facilities will need to have the widest possible
use if our scenic and recreational needs for the future are to be
met. As this occurs, it will be increasingly necessary to balance

conflicting factors to achieve the best use of available opportunities. Provision of the required space for people should be a major consideration.

AREA ELEMENTS: Profile Aspects of Areas

Of the area elements, the agricultural area is the most prolific example of a tilted plane. Fields are useful in delineating the form of terrain. Agricultural form is conspicuous because of three factors: consistency of area surface, distinctions of boundary, and contrast with its surroundings. If the land if fertile and well cared for, the consistency of surface and the contrast it offers to its surroundings will be greatest.

Fig. 60 - Fields help define terrain form.

A newly plowed field, or one whose crop has just been harvested, or one in the middle period of growth of a flourishing
crop, presents a vivid and contrasty relationship to its background. If the land is unused, or ungrazed the surface changes.
Weeds and shrubby growth, unchecked by grazing, mar the uniformity of surface. Fences left in disrepair or the unkept ditches
encourage indistinct boundaries. Careful husbandry increases the
visual contrast; the careless farmer and the abandoned orchard
are responsible for softer, less controlled definition. Abandon-
ment causes the cared-for appearance of the thrifty farm to give
way to a ragged neglected look. The boundary grows tangled and
overstepped with weeds. The intrusions destroy the former contrast. It would be far cleaner visually, to remove all structures
and other man-made traces so that natural recovery would not be
visually degraded by obvious neglect and decay.

Tilted planimetric area elements serve to define the topographic nature of sloping terrain and to attract the attention by
offering surfaces tilted to the light. Sunlight reflected from
ground surfaces varies with the degree of inclination. Various
configurations of surface result in a more interesting pattern
of lighted versus shadowed surfaces.

Other Area Elements

Other area elements which serve as important definers of form
in the Landscape Unit are folded surfaces, curved surfaces, and
warped surfaces. When such surfaces are visible as area elements,
they serve to farther clarify the detailed nature of the ground
surface. The varying tilt surfaces reflect light in variable ways
which permits ridges, profile lines, and other surface irregularities to emerge visually from the neutral area background. Area
elements having folded or broken surfaces can present strong contrasts.

Fig. 61 - Contrasts in surface configuration.

Flat, or nearly horizontal surfaces generally reflect the
greatest amount of light from the sky or clouds. Area elements
which are rolling, curvilinear or curved in profile display

attractive gradations for their lighted surfaces which serve to differentiate their terrain form. These curved surfaces are usually warped to some degree.

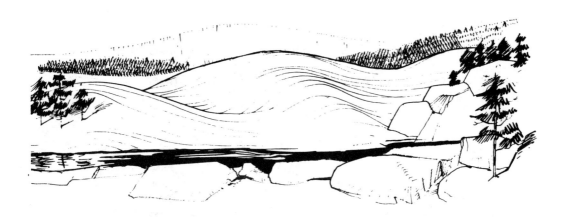

Fig. 62 - Gentle gradations of rolling terrain.

Mass Elements

Mass elements are distinct visual elements. They emerge from their neutral background with clarity. The term "mass" is a deliberate one, meant to suggest the nature of the thing seen and to differentiate it from elements which form the background, the neutral visual ground, or the enclosure of the Landscape Unit.

All mass elements need not be substantial, having actual weight. Our concern is with visual qualities. Negative masses, such as excavations, are fully as massive in visual terms as are mining spoil or massive fills. The principal exception is that positive masses on the surface may evidence a positive profile seen against a bright sky. Such profiles can be very contrasty and hence very compelling. On the other hand, pits or excavations often contain water, or have level bottoms which reflect considerable light. The man-made aspect of mass elements is a prominent characteristic. It is certainly a positive mark which induces visual isolation from natural features. Dams, because of their scale, and our understanding of the tremendous thrust of the water which they resist, are probably the most dramatic of the Mass Elements.

Fig. 63 - Dams are dramatic mass elements.

Fig. 64 - Large highway fills are significant mass elements

Highway construction in the Landscape Unit is often
at a sufficient scale so that engineered fills are a magnitude
comparable with other large mass elements. Canals or major
irrigation system components can be classified as mass elements
of the negative type. Other examples are highway borrow pits,
open face mines, gold dredge tailings, sanitary fills, and fill
structures in water expanses.

Fig. 65 - Canals or excavated waterways as negative mass elements.

Mass elements, positive or negative, are distinctive because they represent a visible intrusion in the Landscape Unit. To some degree, each such element degrades the visual quality by forcing the attention to a part of the environment which is out of fit. The greater the contrast exhibited by the mass element, the more vivid it appears relative to its background, the greater the attraction, the greater the potential degradation by competition. (Kepes, 1949).

The purpose of these remarks is not to diminish the rightful admiration which should be directed to American engineering works. Rather, it is to point out possible alternatives which can prevent the aesthetic imbalance occurring when man-made elements are in competition for our attention in the Landscape Unit. The problem is two-fold. First, it is necessary to decide that certain units of land have important visual qualities. Then it is necessary to use reasonable controls in placing construction elements in such landscapes.

Fill structures which project into the water have little to commend them under the best of circumstances. Even so, a modest attention to avoiding the most blatant and obvious geometric form could improve their visual relationship to their setting. Many visual linkages of color, of plant types, and of form, are possible. Intrusion of such elements into significant view lines can be controlled.

Fig. 66 - Visually compelling fill structures affect natural
          scenic values.

Regular and Irregular Masses

Mass elements may be regular in form, perhaps even rigidly geometric, or they may be irregular. It should be clear that the most perfectly geometric forms are likely to offer the greatest contrast when seen against the natural, usually irregular, background of the Landscape Unit.

Every construction project which results in mass structures, every engineering or architectural structure is adaptable to a variety of forms, within the reasonable functional limits of the problem. Some choices result in mass elements which are economical in structural form and simple in outline. Alternative choices may produce considerably more complex visual forms. Such complex elements may be extremely prominent, visually. Busy forms, elaborate decorative detail, or poor visual linkages with the landscape are all capable of generating a degree of contrast which is intrusive; claimants for attention. Such intrusive mass elements can be destructive of the unity of the Landscape Unit.

Fig. 67 - Construction projects are adaptable to a wide variety of forms.

Irregular mass elements may be more easily concealed against a complex background, particularly if the colors and materials chosen blend with that background. Concealment is a useful way to avoid unwanted contrasts but may not be economical or easy to accept. This course may require considerable extravagence in form and in the quantity of materials required. If forms structurally are simple but made visually complex by embellishment, there is the manifest disadvantage that the visual appearance does not explain the inner structure.

Irregular mass elements are often accidental forms. Deposits of materials from mining, manufacturing or earthwork may be somewhat regular in plan or profile because of the physical actions of the materials being deposited. The total is usually irregular in form. A mass element of this type is simply a happening, a gradual accretion which may be unnoticed because of slow build-up.

Fig. 68 - Mass elements are often accumulations.

Borrow pits of large scale are common near major highway construction. Often these hold runoff water which collects over a
period of time, forming accidental lakes. At times, these are
constructed in the path of a roadside stream so that there is a
ready source of water and a means for flushing stagnant water.
These offer considerable possibilities for dual purpose structures
where both the material removed and the negative structure formed
are of use. (Bauer, 1966).

Many such structures have accidental forms. Removal of
material in an expeditious way is the primary consideration; the
form which results is completely accidental. This is a good example of a casual man-made structure which should be carefully
considered as an object for design. Both the surface form and the
form of barrow pit banks or shores are subject to a great deal of
visual improvement. What may be a degrading intrusion in the
landscape unit can be made functionally and visually enhancing.

Point Elements

Point elements are objects, structures, contrast points or
striking confluences of lines, boundaries, or edges. At the scale
of the Landscape Unit the actual size of these point elements may
be quite large; the scale and the viewing distance often reduces
their apparent size to the equivalent of a point. This point is
too small to require scanning. Its significance can be understood
at a glance, or given greater distances, its detail is too small

to resolve visually. In this case, it becomes formless; a dot or point.

In bland, featureless, or continuously forested landscape, the presence of a point element can be very striking. A very small element of the proper contrast will prove attractive to the eye in a manner completely out of proportion to its size. Contrast is critical. The color of materials chosen, the nature of the visual field or background, the direction and intensity of light, are all important factors. Smooth in contrast to rough, light contrasting with dark, structural contrasted with natural, glittering objects in a dark field; these are other variants which partially describe a number of conditions which may permit point elements to emerge as arresting visual incidents in the Landscape Unit. Such point elements may appear in an endless variety of ways. For simplicity, let us group the possible occurrences into three basic types: isolated points, configurations, and textural groups.

Isolated point elements are those which are removed from other elements by distance, by similarity, by color, by brightness or by other distinguishing marks. They appear as single incidents which are unrelated to other visible items in the scene. If such points are infrequent in a bland landscape, their visual importance may be very great. It is possible to dominate a vista by a single striking point element which attracts the attention of the observer to a degree which is entirely out of proportion to the object.

Man-made point elements are especially striking in a natural setting. There is a fundamental difference between a structural or architectural element which may have a manufactured finish, geometric configuration, and a clear functional purpose from that of the more complex and yet prolific objects in the natural setting. When there are thousands of trees in view, or acres of grassland, or miles of shoreline, one white house, or one transmission pole, or one forest watch tower can be unusually compelling.

There can be little doubt that man is interested in the presence and activities of his fellows. Human achievement has a degree of primacy over nature when we view the visible world. This primacy if often a problem, especially when we wish to concentrate on developing or preserving the visual quality of a landscape or water setting which is predominately natural in character and of high quality. In such scenes, the man-made object is a visual intrusion. It intrudes to claim our interest and attention. Certainly in this sense of intrusion, of interruption, of visual upset, the man-made object is degrading to the place. As society becomes more concerned over the scarcity of natural places which are untrampled or undeveloped, it is evident that isolated point elements which are man-made will be more severely criticized for their degrading presence. Such structures will be very much in the public eye.

If the point elements in the visual field are not arranged in any easily perceptible configuration because of the absence of

a real relationship, surprising things may happen when we attempt
to interpret what we see. It is possible to read meanings into
arrangements which are completely accidental. Chance configurations may occur. We may try to resolve elements which are not
there and which were never intended. Such visual searching is not
likely to end in a positive aesthetic reaction nor is it likely
that this condition can add anything to the landscape unit's
scenic value. Complexity is not the problem. The difficulty is
organization. A multiplicity of visible man-made point elements
which have no organizational rationale will degrade the Landscape
Unit. If such elements are necessary to fulfill functional requirements, then organization -- design -- is visually necessary.

Fig. 69 - Point elements attract the eye.

Enhancement of a landscape unit is possible when there is an
obvious multiplicity of point elements visible. The object is
simply to reduce the obvious nature of these elements, especially
those which may be more prominently located. Reduce the contrast
between object and background, between point element and the landscape unit and the offending element may go away -- visually.
Contrast may be reduced in a number of ways. Changing color by
painting; reducing gloss or reflectivity; planting trees to place
the offending object in shadow; reducing movement and activity near
the point; softening highly visible angularities or structural complexity in favor of less visually exciting outlines -- these are
all common and rather obvious remedies. Removing such elements
from ridgeline positions to reduce the contrast of silhouette;
preventing mirror reflections; adapting structural forms characteristic of local terrain, or rocks; reducing artificial lighting;
keeping clearings or necessary grading to a minimum -- these are
all equally effective but less common possibilities for enhancement by contrast reduction.

In some situations, point elements are very numerous and close
together. They tend to be seen as a pattern of forms, colors, or
objects rather than as isolated forms. Villages, towns, recreational or industrial developments, urban elements -- these are
examples. When the number of elements is large, there is little
which can be done to conceal them all. It is possible, as in the

last example, to reduce the contrast of individual elements but his
is but a small dent in the solution. The best strategy is to make
the overall pattern low in contrast or to use any of the previously
mentioned methods for concealment. The best that can be done is
to contain this type of visual distraction, bring contrast down to
a reasonably common level, and, in the case of new construction,
design the necessary groupings so that a sense of organization
commensurate with the intended function and its setting is a recognizable visual attribute. Purposeful and unified organization
is certainly more enhancing than recognizable disorder or obvious
and complete lack of control.

Point elements are not always static. There are many kinds of
elements which move in the landscape. Any movement makes for a
more difficult problem to solve. Movement is attractive by simple
contrast with the majority of static natural elements.

At the large scale which typifies the Landscape Unit, only
higher speed elements such as automobiles, trains, trucks, or air-
craft move rapidly enough to be readily perceptible. On the other
hand, movement in the foreground of any kind is potentially attractive to vision. The rate of motion at near distances may be
less, and still be of striking interest. Moving people or animals
may be very prominent.

For landscape where natural values are to be given first consideration, vista points should overlook landscape, not roads. Not

only is the road structure degrading to natural qualities, but the
motion of colorful, highly reflective automobiles is unduly compelling. Roads may be concealed by forest, or the vista point may be
a projection which conceals roads behind ridges or sheltering terrain. Man-made moving elements should be considered a major visual
intrusion.

Color and Texture

At large scale in the landscape, color and texture are more
prominently related to the surface of the earth, to crops and plants
and to water, than to man-made elements and structures. The exception, of course, is the area which is highly urbanized or indus-
trialized. Area elements and mass elements of this scale may display
characteristic color or have sufficient surface variety to present
a textured surface.

Color accents function. The contrast between a color element
and its background is the visible reality, not so much the shape or
its size. Violent contrasts of color can be powerful visual incidents which cause sharp differentiation to occur. Incongruous color
accents such as red or orange against the subdued greens of a forest
background are exclamatory. Yellow or orange colors are easily seen
against water. Light, bright color is contrasty against dark backgrounds, and dark color against bright hard light rock or sand.
(Minnaert, 1954).

It is common for us to think of color in functional terms.

Red, as a bright arresting color seen against the modesty of most backgrounds, is familar to all for its warning function. Other colors are used in traffic and for various signals, flags, and signs. Colored lights have various meanings depending on context, form and location. The surface color of materials can be indicative of the nature of that material. For living elements, color suggests the season, age, organic health, and other environmental factors.

Considerable sentiment remains for permitting color to suggest something of the inherent integrity of materials. In fact, for materials which have an inherent resistence to the elements, display of their exposed surfaces is an invitation to recognize the durability of the structure. Common examples are expensive and distinct materials such as slate, marble, or granite. Steel and aluminum have been manufactured which utilize natural corrosion as both a decorative finish and a bar to more extensive and damaging weathering. These uses are a reflection of an established wish to treat material and structure honestly and to permit the process of weathering to deepen the visual expression.

STRUCTURES AND ALTERATIONS IN THE SETTING UNIT

The setting unit is, by definition, a clearly perceptible unit of landscape with its spatial enclosure and boundaries seen from a position on the ground. It is a distinct entity with size varying within wide limits. Examples range from a small shoreside clearing in a heavily wooded region, to an extensive open landscape whose boundaries are terrain features, and through which a watercourse makes it way, or in which a lake is situated. Some examples may have distinct and complete spatial qualities. Others may be relatively open. Some may have a central primary water element. Others may be distinct landscape units important primarily because of their situation on the water. The fundamental considerations are that the setting unit takes its form from those elements which the observer sees from a ground-level position, and that there is a visible, distinct, and defined land area which is significant because of its relationship to the water.

The setting unit may not always be visible from elevated or distant positions. Some setting units may be extensive in size and are, therefore, distinct from distant view points. Significance at times may come from the distinctiveness it enjoys when seen as a distant component of the landscape unit. However, its primary qualities may only be completely appreciated from the observer's position within the unit and while on the ground. At times, the landscape unit and the setting unit may be, or appear to be, one and the same. Such may be the case where the landscape unit is small and the perceptible visual boundary elements are sparse or indistinct. Normally, however, the setting unit is a smaller element of landscape and water which is located within the boundaries of the landscape unit.

The visual distinctiveness of both these units results from the natural conditions of the landscape and the water; man-made elements are secondary in their visual importance. Mountain, forest, and water, are compelling elements; man creates poor competition. When the reality of visual surroundings is catalogued, the scale and primacy of natural conditions is dominant in the formation of significant visual unit areas, landscapes, or waterscapes. Structures, engineering works, and landscape alterations are incidental.

Unfortunately, in some cases which are degrading to the natural scene, man-made developments are potently attractive to the eye, simply because of their contrast to the natural qualities of their surroundings. Mine dumps, tall buildings, towers, piers and other examples, ranging from very small to massive may have an extraordinary visual primacy. The vividness and contrast which are created both by their design and their landscape location directly influence the degree to which they may visually stand out from their backgrounds and, hence, the degree to which they are influential to the whole. In those cases where the natural qualities of landscape and water are judged to be primary, it is important that we find the rationale for designing and locating necessary construction. Access, fire protection, sanitation, and utility construction are important, but careful consideration of their impact must be made.

Linear Elements

The simplest and most obvious of the man-made linear elements
in the setting unit is a line. It is the purest and most functional
form; without real substance, except in the most limited sense.
Normally not intended to be a contributer to aesthetic value, it
has, in fact, a strong influence. As a functional ordering device,
it is endowed with remarkable directive power.

A simple example is a painted line. These are used in countless
ways. As bounding elements, they define the limits of roads, parking
areas, and recreational areas, where the need for a precise boundary
is important. Used on roads to define the centerline, they additionally indicate the presence of road hazards, lines of sight, safety
areas, and passing zones. Steering is a continuing process of linear
visual comparison and reaction; the line of the pavement helps relate
to the line of advance of the vehicle.

As division elements, painted lines are used to apportion areas
into meaningful subdivisions. Parking areas are marked to indicate
the space which is allocated for each vehicle, and the alignment or
directional place of that vehicle with respect to the total
available space. Visitor centers often use such elements to direct
the flow of visitors, define assembly areas or indicate safety zones.
Recreation structures and game courts use them as guides to the
conduct of play.

Painted lines represent definite restraints. They define the agreed-upon limits for human action where personal choice, individually applied, would create a chaotic result. Frequently, legal restraints are related to the presence of such lines, and the manner in which the public behaves with respect to them. Crosswalk lines, and parking zones are familiar examples.

In the most negative sense, such restraining lines are a visual block on the landscape. They force us to perceive restraining patterns. In the best sense, they aid in the visual act, helping us to understand the functional nature of man-made elements and our visual relationship to them. We need them, we become dependent upon them, and usually conduct ourselves seriously with respect to them. Such restraining lines, accordingly gain from us a measure of respect and attention which is entirely out of scale with their physical reality.

Fig. 70 - Painted lines can be compelling.

A paradoxical result of our dependence upon such restraining lines is that we pay more than ordinary attention to them. Considering their size, they become super visual elements. If they are used to proliferation, carelessly, or whimsically, some highly arresting or even grotesque effects become possible. At issue is the manner, the responsibility, and the restraint with which we use them. Some make life easier, safer, and eliminate uncertainty. Others add to the problem of visual confusion and are degrading to the best qualities of landscape.

Fig. 71 - Notices require care in location.

Often, their compelling qualities are exploited in the name of advertising or as figurative elements in decorative designs for buildings, signboards, and interiors. In all these instances, there is a danger of eroding our confidence in the legitimate purposes for directive lines, if their use is cheapened by frivolous application.

Directive Lines

A most important family of linear elements in the landscape
unit are those which provide for linear movement. Roads, paths,
trails, tramways, and railed vehicles are examples. Because we see
such lines, these elements become highly directive. Location of an
attractive path or road which stretches out from the observer's position to some point in the distance is a visual invitation to travel
that way. Such indirect invitations may range from powerful straight
lines which are preemptory in their summons, to gentle winding curves
which invite a slower, softer, and more roundabout way.

Fig. 72 - Paths suggest movement and direction.

The directive function of linear man-made elements is very
important. Roads and paths are but one example, a limited one in
which the observer is guided along a line of advance which is

appropriate to the terrain. Linear elements in other applications
can be used to direct the gaze of the observer to desired points
within the setting unit or to significant view points in the distance. Used with proper restraint and in moderation, this device
permits an inhanced enjoyment of the intrinsic qualities of the
landscape and water by permitting necessary improvement elements
to serve visual as well as purely functional usefulness.

Insensitive use of the directive function can easily become
degrading. The essential rightness of good landscape is a felt
quality but a very real and valuable one. The observer in a good
natural landscape needs little in the way of artificial visual
stimulation. What is best is to arrange the necessary structures
or improvements so that they do not deliberately intrude. This does
not mean that we must hide the things we build or disguise them to
look like log cabins, nor that the main function of introduced
planting is to conceal. Deliberately intruding means to build in a
calculated and heavy-handed manner, using the advantages of the
visual resource in an exploitive fashion. Unfortunately, it is not
widely understood that the process is self-defeating. Poor, cheap,
and thoughless design degrades, not only the landscape, but itself.

Fig. 73 - Thoughtless advertising degrades water values.

The best weapon is the force of example. If public agencies
which have a responsibility for preservation and utilization of our
natural and scenic resources demonstrate sensitivity and restraint,
the education value will more than justify the care and effort required. Cost is secondary; restraint is not related to dollar values.

These considerations require constant vigilance. The presence
of grand scenery has apparent soporific tendencies. Beautiful
natural contrasts seem, at times, to induce a sleepy disregard for
the merits of location, the quality of architecture, or the distraction of conveniences. It may be profitable to reconsider the
old verbal saw which remarks of the woodsman that "he cannot see
the forest for the trees." There is a depth of meaning in that

saying which suggests that, in addition to cutting the occasional
good tree, our axeman clear away some worthless snags.

Edges as Lines

Linear elements are decisively important at the edge or border.
Terminating one material -- one surface -- one quality for another,
this line of juncture is highly significant visually. In no instance is it more meaningful than at the line which marks the meeting
of land and water. This is a dynamic line, borrowing its motion from
the water. It reflects much on the nature of the shore, the shape
of the terrain, and the quality of the water. These natural conditions can create linear water edges which are exceedingly complex
and interesting. The fascinating story of the ascendency of water
on the landscape is present for the inquiring eye and mind to seek
out.

Nature's water edges are both fragile and evocative. They
cannot support even a modest increase in concentrated foot traffic.
Moist soils pack down into dense, hard, and sterile barrens. Low
and delicate plants are trampled. Grasses and flowers will not
survive the compaction. The usual results of such usage are muddy
water-filled pockmarks, dry iron-hard soils, and a trampled, barren
and sterile, visually unattractive degradation of the waterside.

Man must often improve or alter the edge. What he creates out
of necessity should emulate natural qualities, but with a different
kind of expression, related to the means. It is not possible to
recreate nature, by design, except in the most limited ways, or by

the hand of a rare, special genius. In any event, man's problem
is to produce functional, as well as visually handsome elements
which alleviate the conditions detrimental to functional use. A
parallel requirement, and one which we are considering here, is
to avoid visual contamination. Stated in the positive sense, we
must be concerned with making a constructive visual contribution to
the resource. The word enhancing, then refers principally to the
degree to which the elements of the artificial structures of man in-
terrelate to form a visually satisfying unity. The word has a second
important meaning which is the principal consideration of this study.
It refers to the degree of success attained in the visual integration
of required functional elements into the landscape; to the success of
the fit. Two guiding principles are: to emphasize the contrast of
types, and, to subdue the contrast of types.

Artifice and nature are fundamentally contrasting. Assuming
that we hope to encourage the best of each, an emphasis on this inherent contrast of types clarifies the differences between them.
The unspoken assumption is that we will attempt to protect natural
values with structures where man threatens, or has begun, to create
visible deterioration of visual qualities. We attempt to preserve
that which is good in nature, and constructively, to design and
build the best that is possible. Using this guiding principle, it
is best to strive for evocative functional form. This principle
states in the complete converse that structures should not be
imitative or reflective of nature.

Using the second principle, developmental forms may contribute more to the total of scenic values if they are evolved from natural motifs. This means is no more imitative than the first; concrete is not made to suggest rock. Instead, design proceeds from the premise that visual continuity and lack of contrast may be least damaging in a given situation. Using this principle, there is the advantage that nature will be the model for the forms adapted by man.

Which of these suggested principles to use in a given situation is entirely dependent upon the place and its qualities. Only one thing is certain; when use itensifies, artificial means will have to be the instrument which prevents the erosion of desirable visual and natural values.

The edge of the water is a particularly compelling place. It will attract attention out of proportion to its extent. As this happens, it deteriorates more rapidly than higher ground. In places of great scenic interest, highly durable and permanent structures may be the only feasible possibility.

Fig. 74 - Intense use requires durable structure.

A valid planning principle is to avoid impact concentrations
by keeping use as diffuse as possible. Durable linear elements like
paths and trails may be of material assistance by providing changing
views and a larger number of contact points.

Profile Lines

Profiles are a special type of linear element. The profiles of
nature: ridges, mountain outlines, forest silhouettes, and water
horizons, are important definers of the nature and quality of the
natural surroundings. They describe something of the character of
the place which is hidden from us by distance. Small hints are
enough. The characteristic appearance of a Douglas-fir skyline contains little detail but conveys much. The softer, rounded appearance
of the mixed hardwoods on a Massachusetts ridgeline is quite

different. Given a little experience and knowledge, such distant
hints are enough to conjure up a vivid image in the mind of the
viewer. Man-made profiles function in much the same way.

At the medium scale represented by the setting unit, man-made
alterations to the ground surface are decisively important when seen
from ground level. No single aspect of structure is more consistently ignored or neglected than this. When the ground surface has
been disturbed and then reshaped, it can never retain those qualities
and detail which give natural land surfaces coherence. Forms must
be found which give structure positive visual qualities and these
must be related to both the functional requirements of the development and to the need for visual coherence in the natural scene.

The scale of the setting unit permits the perception of line in
elements which are not linear. A common example is found in the
manner in which natural elements are cleared and removed to make way
for improvements. In clearing wooded terrain, cultivating ground to
produce firebreaks, mowing or cutting low plants or grasses for week
control, for fire abatement, or for mowing for neatness: in all these
operations, the linear edge which results is seen in sharp contrast
to adjoining natural areas. Such practices are obviously degrading
because they clearly demonstrate unthinking or careless disregard
for visual values. A little softening of such hard lines can produce a pleasant neutrality of the junction.

Fig. 75.- Prominent clearings result from geometric edges.

When constructing any element which requires clearing the original cover and regrading the surface, a common practice deposits
rubble or trash collections at the edges. These, because of their
tendency to be seen in linear form, become sharply evident.

Fig. 76 - Construction debris often remains on site.

Linear patterns across the landscape is the common result of
road construction to provide access to water. High construction
standards require these edges to be skillfully softened or blended
into the shapes of the terrain. In ordinary work, there is a disregard for most values except engineering and safety. The result
can be disturbing linear interruption -- a structure plastered on
the landscape.

Fig. 77 - Structures should fit the landscape.

When water flows, its profile is evocative of the innermost nature of landscape. Where water is able to dominate, it cuts and grinds its way into the earth. These actions on streambed, shoreline and bank, trace the record of a living force, in periods of strength and in periods of relapse.

The profiles of our landscapes should be made as evocative as the profiles of nature's watercourses. They are evocative of different stresses, however, and therefore must assume different forms. They must demonstrate that man is able to organize and shape his forms to reflect their function, their structure, and their relation to their environment. They should also be evocative so that we can experience pleasure in forms which express these inner qualities as well as more obvious and pleasant externals.

Neglect in ordinary things seems inexcusable. One of the most common is the linear profile form for walks and roads. Highway design is less commonly at fault than are these lesser examples. Engineers use linear profile forms which are geometric. These have smooth visual continuity, a result of the flow or fit of the various geometric components. Mathematical perfection creates a kind of visual quality which is closely related to the qualities of natural scenery. The hidden inner order influences the visible form. In work which can be faulted, orderly profiles are disregarded, structure is "pasted" on the surface, and simple visual pleasure is lost.

Fig. 78 - Casual profiles can be visually destructive.

Fences, the edges of planted areas and other simple elements
are not visually irritating when the profile remains characteristic
of the existing surface. The need for higher order is related to
extent of change as well as to finish, precision, and function.

Fig. 79 - Fences and other minor elements can be more casually
         sited.

Area Elements

Area elements in the setting unit are primarily on the ground
plane. They are distinct areas of open ground with a consistency
of surface, color, form, or function. Alternatively, they may
have a fairly complex surface if their boundary is visually strong
or if the area function is active or important.

Open areas like fields, surfaced parking spaces, clearings,
or beaches are easily distinguishable when their boundaries are distinct, or significant. Areas which are partially covered with trees

or other growth are much less so. These may not appear, in a first
visual survey, as area elements. The presence of people or objects
of visual significance are often compelling enough to tip the scales.
As an example, a portion of lightly forested ground which has no
distinct boundaries and which extends for a considerable distance
may gain area significance by the placement of campsites or picnic
facilities. These elements in strong contrast to the natural setting are highly conspicuous, each makes a potential claim to a
portion of surrounding ground, and the composite total of all such
improvement elements is sufficiently great to set the area clearly
apart.

The elements in the visual scene are quite simply, those elements
which are different. In the town, an isolated tall tree becomes a
famous landmark. On the open plain, the presence of a single human
is conspicuous. Man-made structures are usually the most compelling
objects in sight when they are set in natural landscape. This fact
forces us to practice constant restraint, if we wish to avoid visual
distractions and degrading clutter.

Area elements are, with enclosing and water elements, the most
decisive in establishing visual attraction. When the enclosure, the
water and the area elements are distinct and mutually complimentary,
the result is a place of unusual visual and human interest. (Not
enough is known about the fundamental reasons behind the attraction
man finds in such areas. Specific research is needed. The reality
is clear enough.)

Area elements need not be on level ground. Sloping, warped, and folded terrain may be highly attractive, depending on enclosure and surface. There is, however, added interest in level or favorable ground, probably because one relates strongly to sites which have a potential use, even if this is as modest as walking comfortably. Certainly the conservation of energy is a basic human requirement which is most simple to attain on moderate terrain. When evaluation takes into account the cost and the potential difficulty of locating improvements, level or slightly sloping terrain must be rated higher. From a different point of view improvements on unfavorable ground are likely to be relatively violent in their effect on existing natural elements and may, therefore, degrade existing values.

Area relationships are linked with definite human purpose. If not serving a specific functional need, areas have a visual unity which helps form part of the character of the place and gives it form and extent. In water landscapes, most setting units will have been created by natural means. Clearings, meadows, beaches, sheltered coves, and pleasant banks adjacent to water are examples. In the classification of natural water resources, likely candidates for this designation will emerge naturally, as they prove attractive, or useful or have a particular historic or functional significance.

The setting unit is also the primary location for structures and landscape changes which may be required to fulfill functional requirements. Human activity will center here. When development takes place, the number and kinds of structures and activities may be

large, certainly the level of change to the natural landscape will
be far greater than elsewhere. This complexity leads to the most
elusive, yet important quality of unity which must be a basic
objective of design in the setting unit. In order that activity
improvements relate well to natural elements, they should be seen
as part of a unified and integrated developmental whole, rather than
as isolated, contrasting, and probably disturbing elements.

No matter how perfectly these created elements may be disposed
or unified in their arrangement, it requires a considerable degree
of restraint to resist placing improvements in a visually forward
position from which there is a challenge to the primacy of natural
values. Our basic purpose is to protect our visual resources by
reasonable means. If the resource is lost, the need for improvements
is gone. To this end it is usually less prejudicial to natural order
to make improvements recessive in their visual prominence. Restraint
in the application of garish colors is a virtue. Blatant advertising
signs can be made modest. Freak architectural styles need be used
less in natural settings than in the competitive city. Electric
laundries, frozen foods, movie screens, rental boats, and water
skiing may be popular with a majority of the public but they add
little to the basic qualities which attract us to the place. If
such amenities are more desired than scenery, they should be located
in places of low natural scenic value or in places where comparable
scenic advantage can be created by design. Only a forthright stand
on this point will prevent the eventual reduction of a substantial
portion of priceless natural values.

Enclosing Elements

The most distinct form of man-made enclosing elements is the vertical. Planting trees is a simple means to achieve such enclosure using natural materials. An alternate to planting is the selective cutting of certain plants or trees to achieve a stronger, more visually distinct element. If crudely done cutting can create stark clearings which are visually detrimental to landscape quality continuity. Such alteration may also transform ecological conditions. Cutting exposes the previously shaded forest floor, reveals unsightly lower foliage which is dead or stunted because of previous shade, and opens the forest to new wind damage. Ecological imbalance rights itself by reaction. It is to be expected that such extreme changes will stimulate natural reaction and produce new, alien visual conditions.

Conversely, careful selective removal of dead and diseased plants may benefit the formation of a stronger, more distinct visual entity in the setting unit. It may be possible to improve distant water and landscape views. Some improvement in watershed function may be possible. With care, a considerable amount of such removal may have little effect on the predominate visual qualities. When fire, windstorm, or disease have been absent, such practices may be sound management, visually and ecologically.

Most constructed enclosure is the vertical type. Fences or screens are sharply visible examples. At setting unit scale, vertical

208

elements are important to define area elements, to function as
directive elements, and to screen undesirable elements. Although
the walls and roofs of buildings are not primarily constructed as
enclosing elements, they can function in this way and often act
as especially solid visual controls.

Fig. 80 - Buildings function as enclosing elements in the setting
          unit.

The use of highly regular forms and arrangements intensifies
the problem of detrimental or degrading use of man-created vertical
elements. They are in stark contrast to the landscape; located or
formed with no regard for the forms or terrain of the setting unit.
Irregular arrangement is less vivid than regular, curves are less
prominent than straight lines, conformity with gradients less a
problem than dead level, and planted enclosure less vivid than structure.

209

Enclosing Configurations and Masses

Altering the ground surface by cutting or filling may be required in order to construct a functional facility, or to visually unify a portion of a setting unit. When this is necessary, the sense of enclosure may be intensified by adopting a more strongly enclosing form. Negative forms like bowl shapes are better in this regard than positive shapes. Valley versus ridge is nature's counterpart argument. The result will be strongest when the form is highly controlled and regular.

Fig. 81 - Landscape and water in an enclosing configuration.

Leveled ground is conspicuous in relation to the varied topography of natural surfaces. It is best to avoid dead level alterations. These are visual standouts which suffer as well from poor drainage. Often, a dead flat surface will appear to be curved because of the force of its surroundings. Visual illusions can be

responsible for oddly detrimental appearnace qualities. These may
be avoided by foresight and the adoption of countermeasures.
(Luckeish, 1922).

Careful reconstruction of the disturbed ground surface is
normally necessary. Often, complex forms are required. The shape
of roads are different from turf or cultivated area. Slopes or
banks which connect natural areas from altered ones become distinct
and separate parts. Buildings require a special treatment for proper support and for drainage.

The ideal objective is to recreate the surface so that it becomes as continuous as possible -- natural areas flowing easily into
created areas. This conception allows for surface differences; these
are obviously required. However, the margins of both surfaces and
enclosure carefully avoid extreme contrasts which are unattractively
detrimental.

Plants may be introduced as complex configurations or as masses
in order to perform enclosing functions. This is a variant from the
use of trees or higher plants as vertical enclosure. Such elements
may have several types of distinguishing characteristics, anyone of
which may be appropriate in a given situation. As mass they are
less precise in the defining function than taller trees but such
masses may be composed of a complex of plants to serve a visual or
ecological purpose. They may effect repairs to an important ecotone.
They may provide shelter from wind for permanent plantings. It may

be necessary to repair natural damage from flood or windstorm. Blossom
or fruit can provide a visual point of interest. Textural differences
between leaf types offer relieving contrasts.

Enclosing elements classified in this study as enclosing configurations or composite structures are earth, rock, concrete, or
wood structures not fundamentally vertical in form. Examples are
mounds, amphitheatres, seats, barriers and edgings. Combinations of
materials are common. Forms may vary from surface configurations to
low structures. Overhead shelters, slope treatments, and earth
terraces are examples of elements which are not vertical.

Implied enclosure refers to the least confining of the above
types of elements. Subtle gradation of the ground surface is perfectly capable of conveying a sense of enclosure when other, stronger
limiting elements are absent. In the presence of stronger spatial
limiters, these subtle modifying elements may promote a sense of visual
complexity and richness. Most site improvements are combinations of
topographic change and structure. The visual integration of both is
an essential factor in attaining a unifying conception.

There is a visual tendency to string scattered or diverse elements
together, to reorganize forms and patterns in a complex visual field,
to order varied and separated things into new or recognizable formations. Use of this visual tendency permits overlapping functions and
the possibility of suggesting enclosure using modest means. Constant
vigilance is necessary to avoid placement of elements which create an
unintended visual result: inadvertent messages in alphabet soup.

Mass elements, classified as both positive and negative types, are intended to describe landscape forms seen as isolated elements of considerable substance. Large mounds are a good example, too compact to serve as area elements and not the major enclosure in a setting unit. Mine dumps, spoil deposits from grading, refuse, and heaps of raw materials such as coal, salt, or wood refuse are examples of positive elements. Quarries, borrow pits, locks, canals, and caves represent negative examples.

Some such forms: dikes, canals, and ditches, are linear. These may have a directive function as do other linear elements. In some cases, these linear elements may be so disposed that they become enclosing elements. Despite these exceptions, mass elements are distinct in their setting and may be difficult to relate to a unified concept.

A specially destructive type of mass element is that produced by massive shovels or dredges which take up rock or soil in their path, process or sort it, and spew the unwanted debris out on the land as gigantic mechanical excreta. Frequently, the economics of such operations require that extractions be practiced on such a scale that destruction is measured in square miles. Such practices result in mass elements of staggering magnitude on which the existing soil structure is destroyed, all living plants are ground under, and which may never soften to conform to the setting unit which it so violently degrades.

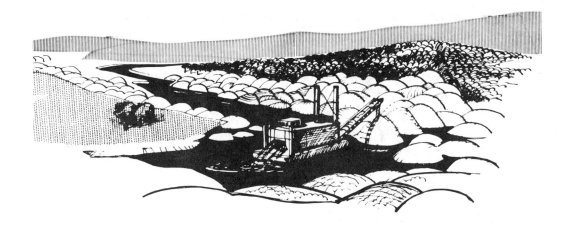

Fig. 82 - Dredging produces unsightly mass elements.

The more regular the form, the greater the contrast. Highly irregular, articulated, or meandering mass elements may be partly concealed by planting or grading but will retain considerable visual impact.

A dam is a conspicuous example of a mass element. Dominating the setting unit, it contrasts with its natural surroundings in material and color, and is so large that no concealment of its mass, or shade on its surface will reduce its visual impact.

Point Elements

Point elements in the setting unit are those man-made elements which are relatively small, are of high contrast, and tend to be seen as an isolated point or unit. A monument, a tower, a flag pole, a piling; these are simplistic examples. Piers, floats, a boat, a house or barn, are larger examples.

Scale is a factor. In large setting units, smaller point elements may disappear in a complex background unless they are extremely contrasty. At a distance, buildings will be seen as definite point elements, even though they may be part of another configuration at close range.

Man-made structures are more easily classified as point elements than are natural objects like trees or outcrops. They are usually formed of artificial materials and conspicuously colored. They are very conspicuous in a natural setting -- attract the attention in a pointed way.

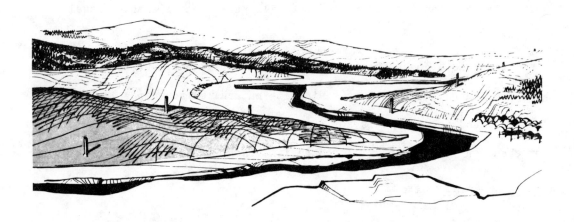

Fig. 83 - Point elements are often conspicuous and orderly in arrangement.

Point elements need to be carefully ordered. Many isolated visual attractions are unduly diverting. If point elements are properly related to other things, it is possible to use them as a means to focus

the attention: to "lead they eye" in an informative and organizational manner, and to add minor enriching accents.

A single point element used as a marker may have a visual significance quite out of keeping with its size or function. When
appropriate, such elements may be valuable in marking significant
places in the landscape without resorting to degrading signs or
other directional devices.

Fig. 84 - Point elements serve as markers.

When a number of point elements are in view, there is a tendency
for the observer to look for clues to the connecting thread which
binds them together. At times, this continuity or connection is obvious, as in the example of a power line or glimpses of road visible
through trees. Such point elements form a single configuration which
is linear. It is not necessary that all the components be visible;

many may be concealed. All that is required is that a sufficient number of structures conform to a perceptible configuration.

The simpler the configuration the more easily it will be resolved. Straight lines, curves, geometric forms are all relatively easy to see and understand, even though there may be substantial parts missing or obscured. We are able to assume continuity even in the absence of many elements and in spite of considerable visual distortion which is the result of our angle of view. A line of elements which traverse relatively complex topography is actually seen to be anything but orderly; but the fact of its linearity is assumed and used as a basis for evaluation. Having made such assumptions, we use them conversely to evaluate topography, or distance, or slope, or any other relationship which we are trying to understand.

Fig. 85 - Point elements can suggest external forces disruptive of natural values.

Color and Texture

In the setting unit color on man-made structures is normally intended to be unifying, bringing widely disparate forms and materials together, but it may have the opposite function; that of identifying or marking significant elements. Color used this way creates a point of color contrast and may lead to the creation of a point element. Structures are sharply contrasting by the simple nature of their origin. Color can serve to reduce such contrasts where desired, or to intensify visual difference.

Cultural practices or irrigation induce differences in the color of natural materials which are most significant. Agricultural land presents a seasonal panorama of color, dependent upon the crop, the location, and the agricultural technique. These are pleasant and informative color differences, but are normal to the nature of an agricultural operation. What may not be foreseen however, is the effect a small amount of water can have in changing the color characteristics of a dry landscape. Intense use often demands more durable and self-renovating surface areas than nature provides. Irrigation and cultivation, fertilizing and mowing help to provide grass areas which resist erosive use and readily recover from overuse. The visual effect, however, may be a problem. It is likely that cultivation will create a marked contrast to existing natural conditions.

It is probable that most observers are not offended by well-kept cultivated areas, particularly turf. What is certain is that such intensive horticulture is essential for heavily-worn ground. The

point at issue is the degree to which the special horticultural
measures necessary are kept in check. Excess water can seep into
neutral ground, creating an accidental green zone. Plants which
are prolific seeders can infiltrate the region with their offspring.
Unwelcome pests may accompany seed, soil, or plant introduction.
Visually, these inadvertencies create degraded fringe conditions
and breed a disunifying crowd of horticultural hangers-on.

Color masses and patterns in the setting unit are commonly
limited to natural materials. When a large number of structures
are present their colors may visually fuse. Urban settings form
characteristic patterns in which color is a factor, contrasting
with the colors of natural landscape.

Textural pattern seen at long range is often the pattern created
by the distribution of structures on the land. Close up, patterns
in brickwork, shingles, or stone add richness to surfaces. The
distribution of window openings or the spacing of pilings in water-
edge developments have similar effect.

STRUCTURES AND ALTERATIONS IN THE WATERSCAPE UNIT

Linear Elements

Waterscape units are classified as those combinations of water and landscape in which water is the key element and where there is unity, or continuity, of a specific, identifiable visual character. Landscape is as important as the water receptacle, and for its influence on the scenic quality of the whole: however, in this classification, the landscape contribution is limited. There are no land areas of significant extent, enclosed or sheltered, of easy terrain. Such ground is limited to minor shore areas. Alternatively, there may be extensive stretches of level or easy ground bounding the water but with a lack of significant enclosure of boundary, whether plants, terrain, or created structure.

Waterscape units may be extensive, depending upon the size of the water body. There may be extensive segments with coherent visual character. Some stretches of river flow for miles without change in the character of the landscape. For preliminary classification, waterscape units may be designated which are the larger part of a stream course or lake. If greater detail is required, divisions may be identified by character differences in the water, coherence of shoreline, continuity in plant cover, or scenic attraction, to mention a few possibilities.

Linear man-made elements in the waterscape unit are of two basic types. Primary are linear structures or elements which are parallel.

to the flow of water or the shore: secondarily, there are those
which cross the stream, lake, or river, or project outward from
the shore.

Edges and Margins

The water's edge is certainly the most evocative zone of all.
Especially striking close up, it has long range visual effect as
well. The influence of water on the edge of the land creates distinct visual color and foliage zones which are visible at the scale
of the setting unit and the landscape unit.

Water makes the edge vulnerable. It saturates and softens
soil, erodes fragile bank structure, and is the central reason for
populations of lush and tender plants. These are delicate conditions which are readily destroyed or degraded by human use,
fluctuating water levels or contamination. Guarding against such
pressures is doubly difficult because of the magnetic attraction of
the water's edge. The fragility and abundant life at this rim is
part of the visual interest; surging motion is another. Earth's
primary interface; creation of green life and grinder of mountains.

When traffic increases, preservation is very difficult. Compaction, trampling, and visible wear are the first indicators.
Almost every waterbody except those with a rocky or sand shore, or
those in remote reaches, exhibit the characteristic imprint of man's
attraction for the edge of the water. A path or concentration of
wear can be found close to the shore. At favorable spots, access
wear records the passage of feet or vehicles. Damage is not

deliberate. It occurs as a gradual dimension of values; the in-
evitable result of an inexorable attraction. Few shore zones can
withstand the pressure of such traffic concentrations. Some type
of linear protective structure is necessary.

Examples of such structures are walls, levees, paved path-
ways, embankments and bulkheads. When these are constructed to
withstand the imposed wear and are kept in good repair, the result
visually is better than a badly eroded, compacted, or muddy natural
edge. While it is certain that an intact water margin can seldom
be improved by structure, design can make possible a sensitive relationship between both landscape and water and will certainly enhance a deteriorated edge.

Reservoirs with fluctuating water levels located in attractive
natural landscapes present problems at the edge for which no universal solution is apparent. The best visual condition which can be
expected is that the shore exposed during drawdown be free of dead
plants, debris, or trash, or composed of bare rock or sand. This
zone is usually a striking linear element which seriously degrades
natural qualities. Proper edge structure to alleviate this condition
is impossible unless the fluctuation in level is slight.

If multiple use is to be encouraged on fluctuating reservoirs
and natural appearance is a desireable factor, it may be necessary
to provide additional high use zones which are separately controlled
so that water levels may be kept at an acceptable mark for a longer

seasonal period. Only in this way can the essential visual qualities
of the shore margin bear a reasonable resemblance to natural qualities.

Many sport and recreation enthusiasts are primarily concerned
with access to water surface for boating, fishing, swimming, or water
sports. For these functions, levee-type paved banks, gangways, ramps,
floating piers, or marine railways may provide physical access and
shore protection. Most such devices are unattractive in a fluctuating
setting, serving well only in a functional sense. Few sporting enthusiasts would prefer a fluctuating pool of a given quality to a
stable one if a choice were available. Attractive and meaningful
surroundings add pleasure to any sport.

As the need for the development of new power and water supplies
increases, the problem of protecting natural values along watersheds
suitable for reservoir storage will be greater. American concepts
of the multiple use of water-centered resources is not very old, nor
is such use widespread in application. We have enjoyed a relatively
plentiful supply of natural lakes and streams for experiences of
natural beauty and for recreation. In recent years, population pressure has forced the use of some scenic and recreational water resources for drinking and irrigation. The resulting dams, distribution
structures, or power facilities have reduced previous natural qualities. Multiple use is essential for a good portion of our water
resources but we must provide against a serious erosion of existing
scenic resources in the process. New research is needed which

relates scenic and recreational use to possible contamination
and pollution.

Retention of natural values is not likely to come as a result
of improving the education of the public. American mobility, the
need for scenic relief from urban surroundings, and the competition
for scarce public facilities will militate against the very high
levels of self restraint which an arrest of present trends would
require. Rational access, areas closed for regeneration, stern new
statutes and limiting measures, such as high use fees, will be
required.

There is promise in planning for greatly increased levels of
attendance and development at certain carefully selected locations
which may be capable of withstanding intensive use. Natural re-
siliency of rocky or sandy areas, forexample or better development
and management procedures could permit a higher impact level without damage.

Linear structures at the water margin which may establish
improved durability are also capable of significant relationships
to both landscape and water. Alternatively linear development
of the edge can force a division between the water and the sur-
fouding landscape. Dikes and levees are examples of this improvement type. What is often creates is a shelf, a plateau or
space near the water, which is cut off from the land by the

Fig. 86 - Durable shore access can help prevent erosion.

structure. Structures which succeed in dividing the landscape into separate bits are not likely to prove as successful as alternatives which provide visual continuity.

Fig. 87 - Water control structures can be barriers.

An important linear element in the waterscape unit is the access
road. Because of the relative ease of constructing roads on valley
floors or near the flow line of streams, many watercourses of scenic
value are in sight or sound of a road. When construction is contem-
plated adjacent to scenic water resources, screening which permits
minimum disturbance by sight or sound should be a fundamental design
requirement. There will be frequent opportunities to bring the
water resource in sight of the road for the benefit of travelers.
This can be done with a minimum of disturbance to natural values
provided that advantage is taken of elevated or screened contact
points.

Area Elements

The most significant area element in the waterscape unit is
that segment of the water which assumes area form. Quiet water,
wide pools, expanses of shore, wide tidal reaches; all are examples. Beach zones, marshy fringes, low banks or shore areas
which are relatively minor elements when viewed separately usually
form the logical edge.

A secondary area element peculiar to waterscape units is primarily linear; the narrow continuous shoreline strip. Classified
as an area element rather than linear because of its openness, and
its strong shore and water boundaries, it serves as an important
visual attraction at the water's edge as well as a means for movement in the absence of roads or developed paths.

Fig. 88.- Foot circulation is important in shoreline strips.

An area element common only to waterscape units is that composed entirely of water with its enclosure or boundary formed by aquatic plants.

Fig. 89 - Waterscape area bounded by aquatic plants.

Three Types of Areas

These are the three basic types of waterscape area elements:
first; water segments which are characteristically different from
the parent body, often with sufficient distinction of rare special
names like "Sawmill Pool" or "49-mile Rapids" or "Alder Flat,"
second; linear shore configurations which provide narrow access and
continuity, third; water surfaces with strong aquatic plant boundaries.

Man-made area elements are very limited in this waterscape unit
classification. Pronounced effect may be caused by fill in the water
in the form of a point, an island, or peninsula, or by a structure.
A gain of usable level space is the usual purpose. Concentration of
use is the consequence making it very difficult to treat, plant,
protect, or maintain the structure in its visual relationship to
natural conditions. The characteristic result is a sharply contrasting intrusion.

Islands or sharp promontories as area elements are of unusual
visual interest. They are also magnetic in their attraction for
boating enthusiasts. Creations of such elements is an excellent
means for attracting attention to an adjacent shore. These may
produce a satisfactory naturalistic addition to the visual resource
if islands can be restricted in use. If restriction is not feasible,
it is better to create a frank artificial structure, designed to
endure under intense use. Piers and floats in waterscape units are
examples. Because such solutions accept heavy use, it may be

possible to ease problems at nearby fragile areas.

The permanent look of a fill, enclosing dike, or cofferdam is visually difficult. However, if permanence permits the generation of significant values such as planted wind screens and useful space, the long range gains may be considerable. Decision will hinge on use intensity. No natural, or artificially naturalistic shore will withstand concentrated use pressure without serious deterioration.

When a reasonably natural appearance is required and use intensity is high, the best visual solution is one which provides a durable edge structure and landscape transition from edge to main shore areas.

Floating structures as waterscape area elements seldom exploit the advantages of that situation. It is possible to use less complex, less expensive structural methods and materials because of the aura of impermanence. Biodegradable is a suggestive word. Ramshackle structures, gay colors, and informal design arrangements are part of a charming informality. Wave motion, reflections and wind flapped flags compel human interest. Such floating contact points with water offer a gay, inexpensive, and surprisingly durable means of accommodating an increase in use without corresponding increase in shore deterioration.

Structures on pilings share the advantage of detachment from the shore edge for high use situations and show most of the visual

advantage of floating structures. The popularity of pier scenery
and recreation attest to the possibilities.

Enclosing Elements

Enclosing elements in the waterscape unit have three primary
subdivisions: the shore or bank qualities which close in the water
surface, the riparian or shore plant cover, and the enclosing
terrain forms. The degree of enclosure offered by these types can
vary from very slight to dramatic. In flat terrain, low banks and
sparse riparian vegetation are quite sufficient to provide enclosure.
Mountain streams may have enclosing mountain walls which are
scenically noteworthy to the degree that the stream itself is a
minor part of the landscape.

If the shore or bank happens to be a man-made element, it
may be a sharply distinct element which dominates the water quality.
Often the means necessary for the construction of bank improvements,
dikes, levees, or enbankments are such that they cause major dis-
turbances to the water element. Mining of gravels for construction
can be responsible for the complete alteration of stream character.
Felling of trees to promote more efficient flows create water
barriers and the anomoly of a plantless landscape by the water.
Heavy equipment used in this work creates havoc along fragile water
margins. These effects are in addition to the usual sterility
of form characteristic of this type of structure

There is every good reason to encourage variations in the disposition and form of structures which are functionally necessary
but which, by their presence in a scenic waterscape unit, degrade
that resource to a marginal point. Variety of structural solution
need not be detractive of functional requirements; a handsome shore
can be made to function as well as a barren ditch. Plants help to
anchor soil and some focal recreational uses will be useful as a
means of concentrating activities and facilities to a practical
degree. The presence of groups of people enjoying themselves is a
useful visual magnet which can be used to concentrate attention to
areas which can be made more useful and durable.

Natural enclosing elements are irregular in form. The quality
and the distribution of soil, the variable availability of water
for plant growth, the local variations in sun and shade, wind,
animals, and old age; all these and more are responsible for variable form and distribution of enclosing plants. The rocks and
mountains respond over time to different variables but the composite of terrain and plants is marvelous irregularity of form,
distribution, and character.

Man alone, is capable of creating complex regularity at landscape scale. Natural elements reveal a few notable exceptions.
Dry lake beds are more plane than man could make them at their
scale. Water obeys the laws of gravity to form vast wet plains

which defy duplication. At another scale, the wonderful and complex figures of leaf, and blossom, and seed; in the regularity of
plant branching habits, and the duplication of species we may see
nature's innermost regularity and order. But for a few exceptions,
the arrangement of the elements of nature one to the other, their
distribution over the face of the landscape, obeys a natural,
ecological regularity, not the visual condition which man is able
to arrange.

The natural and irregular distribution of plants which act
as vertical enclosure along natural streamcourses is a pleasant
characteristic of such waterscapes. When improvement or structure
is necessary, we can emulate these natural qualities to a considerable degree by selecting alterations to remaining plants, by
planting new specimens, or by thinning for effect. Engineering
regularity may be pleasant to see in structures; natural irregularity makes a better counterpoint.

Fig. 90 - Natural plant enclosure provided a pleasant counterpoint
in the waterscape unit.

The major man-made enclosing elements in the waterscape unit
are embankments thrown up to prevent flooding on adjacent land,
protective structures to contain erosion by floodwater, and piers,
bulkheads, or levees which provide access to water or boats and
prevent shipping damage to the land. Such constructed enclosing
terrain or structure is rarely enhancing when compared to natural
values. If the work is performed in response to existing deterioration, its appearance may be an improvement, particularly
in settled or urban areas where few natural qualities survive.

The major and pressing problem is to contain the spread of
more such degrading elements into landscapes which enjoy major
scenic qualities. A great deal can be done by planning. In the

matter of flood control projects of many types, it is possible to
see the onset of problems long before the actual conditions arise
which necessitate repair or water protection. The example of the
Los Angeles River is but a particularly graphic instance of the
fate which is the future of American rivers and streams if better
education of the public and better advance planning are not employed soon. It is not necessary to destroy all our streams by con-
verting them into highly efficient water disposal channels but it
will require cooperation on a scale seldom practiced today. Forests
and open lands must be managed so as to conserve and contain water.
Urban plans must explore new ways for water to be reintroduced into
the soil rather than efficiently piping it away for disposal. By-
pass tunnels or unobtrusive channels can be planned which will permit the scenic values of existing streams to be used, while permitting dispersal of flood waters. No new technology is required,
simply a resolve that the visual world which we require is important,
that we get on with saving what we can of that which remains.

Mass Elements

Mass elements are not so prevalent in the waterscape unit as
in others. Because the waterscape is primarily related to the water
surface and the shore, the mass elements found there are extensions
from the shore -- fills, causeways, water crossing approaches,
breakwaters, jetties, or the like -- or they are fills isolated
from the shore -- islands. Whether peninsular projections or
islands, these mass elements are highly contrasted with their water

setting by the nature of their materials and by their relation to
the water surface. Negative mass elements are not found in waterscape units.

Point Elements

Point elements are numerous in the waterscape unit. Shallow
streams, in particular, contain countless objects of visual interest.
Stones of varied shapes, snags, driftwood, aquatic plants, and the
water itself attract the eye in pleasant profusion. For such streams,
a significant characteristic is the busy and variable attractiveness
of the items which are affected by the water action.

Man-made elements are among the most common contrasting incidents. Pilings, bits of debris, navigation elements, boats, pipe
outfalls: all these are examples of elements seen as individual
items which sharply contrast with their water surroundings. Seldom
are these organized into a meaningful or pleasant pattern. Often
they are things which were used to solve a particular problem which
was unrelated to other problems and devised by a specialist with an
eye to a narrow aperature. A single pole driven into a lake bed to
provide mooring for a boat may offer only minor distraction. That
pole, with four others serving navigational purposes, and five others
for additional moorings, and a dozen remnants of pier supports, can
make a specialized kind of visual pollution at the shoreline.

The difficulty of removing old structures, or fishing out debris,
taken together with the preservative action of water on wood makes
for unusual persistence of point elements which have had their day.

Many degraded shorelines could be simply improved by concerted effort to remove such useless items.

Fig. 91 - Single point elements can be magnetic visual attractions.

Point elements are designated in the classification as isolated points, as linear organizations, and as groups of single elements. Single isolated point elements such as buoys, or pilings, have been mentioned above. Linear organizations are common along shorelines; particularly vivid are the examples formed by piling supports for piers, railroad roadbed supports, fish traps, and the like. Often these are decaying remnants of former structures, a menace to navigation as well as pollution of the visual scene. Such supports may be commonly found in the grouped form. Either the elements are placed in a grouped configuration for some functional purpose, or the observer tends to gather together a number of otherwise random

single elements as a part of the visual act. In either case, these
are seen as groups of things.

In design terms, grouping or other, alternative arrangements
of single elements is a basic part of the problem of producing a
coherant visual organization. Isolated elements must be made to be
part of a total configuration or, alternatively, subdued in their
contrast so as not to disturb major features or qualities of the
remainder. Paradoxically, there is a contradiction in the obvious
fact that some waterfront scenes are best described as "charming."
Often these are places with great profusion of isolated visual
elements. The explanation which comes readily to mind is that the
water body is a great unifier; smoothing over sharp visual contrasts,
forming highly variable patterns of reflections and wave forms, and
touching all with tidal wet, algae green, or water scour. Investigation is needed on the significant visual qualities of confusing
but otherwise compelling visual scenes.

Color and Texture

Color in the waterscape unit functions as suggested in the
classification; color as an accent, color in large area configurations
or masses, and color seen in patterns. Color applied to structure
can be advancing or recessive, depending upon the color and its background. It can be an effective means for isolating elements of some
significance, subduing numerous structures which otherwise would
contrast in a dominating way, and adding vibrant visual interest to
necessary functional structures.

Perhaps the water surface with its constantly changing surface
quality needs to be regarded as the major element which displays pattern. Wave action, the reflective patterns which are altered by the
wind, wave action, and the light, and patterns of color which derive
from both sky and bottom are some of the major textural qualities which
give water its fascination. As texture refers to granularity, weave,
coarseness, or sheen, so the water displays these conditions as it in-
teracts with other environmental forces. The plants, the rocks, and
the mountains also display similar sets of convergences and relationships
which help us to know and understand the underlying nature of the visual
scene. The textural qualities of the Birch tree and those of the Hemlock help us to know our landscape and the relationship of the waterscape to its benign influence.

Fig. 92 - Reflective patterns in the waterscape unit.

EVALUATION OF MAN-MADE STRUCTURES

AND ALTERATIONS TO THE WATER-ORIENTED LANDSCAPE

Diversity of both form and function are common to made elements in the water-oriented landscape. The foregoing descriptive classification of the visual components of such elements suggests this diversity, although the emphasis is on visual form rather than form which derives from functional requirements. Stress has been placed on simplifying the terms which can be used to describe actual situations as well as proposals and to avoid jargon and specialized expressions. It is clear that evaluation and classification will be undertaken by many types of persons, some without previous specialized training. Hopefully, this classification, and the language used to describe it, will be generally clear and will prove a useful tool for those who must produce practical results in field situations.

This evaluative section requires that the classification of elements previously proposed be restructured slightly so that the emphasis is on the consequences of form, rather than on the form itself. In other words, we have described the tomato, now we shall explore its uses in a salad. In the end, what is important is the functional effect various aspects of the visual scene will have on the overall quality of the place, the development, or the resource.

The word "function" is being used here in two distinct senses. The first is that use of the word which applies to physical function.

Roads, for example, must be a minimum width if cars are to pass, must have curvatures which may be negotiated, and must be sufficiently durable to stand up to wear. In the second sense of the word, and again using our example, roads which work well may not be visually expressive of that function; may not look as though they work well. It is not easy to separate these meanings because the highest design forms characteristically address both problems, but the root of a great deal that is wrong with our visual world can be found in the philosophy: if it works it must be good. This evaluation is primarily concerned with applications of the second definitional sense; investigation of the consequences of visual form, the functional consequences as they affect visual quality.

If a typical problem is considered in detail, there are an infinite number of solution configurations which will serve. The right one will depend upon the individual designer. In terms of making a thing work, however, there are important limiting requirements. Each problem will have its own unique needs and these will have to be the basis for subsequent detailed decisions of form or placement, even though detail of form or variability of placement may be an individual response.

The evaluation words used herein are those which apply almost universally to all problems. In order that this be so, they tend to represent broad generalistic visual functions rather than detailed: universals rather than specifics. There is no pretense that the list includes all the possible, or even all the common, considerations of this sort. Rather, the selection of evaluative

terms was chosen from those which would ordinarily not be part of

the vocabulary of the non-design evaluator. He will have sound

personal ideas about beauty, function, and suitability. He may

not be familiar with many of the other important concepts which are

part of the formative process for designers and which can be used

to separate and value aesthetic qualities.

Summary of Proposed Visually Functional Evaluative Terms Relating
To Man-made Structure and Site Design in the Water Oriented Landscape

1. Unifying. To bring together visually, a diversity of perceived

   elements so that each contributes positively to a unified whole.

   Conversely stated, there must be no significant visual disruption

   which can be attributed to an element of the design.

2. Focal. The visual qualities which permit the focus of attention

   to important or desired portions of a landscape or water view.

3. Enclosing. That quality or arrangement which permits a definite

   and limiting enclosure to be formed.

4. Organizing. An arrangement of elements which is structured so as

   to form a coherant pattern, sequence, direction, form, or quality.

5. Enhancing. Arrangements or improvements which prevent the

   visual isolation of disruptive elements or which, by the use of

   new elements, reduces the negative visual impact of existing elements

   or conditions. That arrangement or strategy which visually alters

   the elements in significant ways to relate or constructively

   dissociate.

Description of the Evaluative Terms: Man-made Structure and Site Design in Water Oriented Landscape

Unifying

This descriptive term is one which is at the center of consideration in any design problem. It refers to the tendency of the perceptible visual elements to become mutually complementary. In such circumstances, the totality becomes greater than the simple sum effect of the isolated parts. More precisely, it means that there is a definite functional purpose to the form and disposition of elements; a purpose which is positive as it promotes a larger than life totality.

It is possible to utilize the negative approach. In certain bland or featureless water landscapes, it may be required that some elements be made visually significant, out of proportion to the rest, in order that the elements of a design add the visual significance which a functional solution requires. Not all of the world of nature is attractive. Certain uses will require attractiveness if they are to succeed and all those which are created to perform a definite useful role will have such requirements.

If we are to save the most beautiful, unique, and significant of our natural water landscapes, we must limit the use which their quality stimulates. A positive means to this end is the deliberate creation of additional attractive resources so that the pressure of use may be diluted. This can be done without destroying significant natural values in most cases, especially where natural values are presently marginal. Unless practical alternatives are available or unless rationing is practiced soon, a purist approach to preservation will surely spell the destruction of our best resource.

Focal

Focal is a descriptive term used here to indicate the tendency for man-made elements to become outstandingly significant, noticeable, or attention getting. It is a positive quality; the absence of the focal attribute means visual neutrality, or at the opposite extreme from focal, visually recessive, indistinct, or camoflaged.

Obviously, not all visual elements should be competing for attention. In the water-oriented landscape, water is usually the primary element of interest. In other places, landscape features, water features, or natural color, configuration or form will dominate. In places where natural and man-made elements are both visually significant, focal qualities need to be carefully controlled and limited. Chaotic and disruptive visual competition is easily possible.

The positive and constructive consequence of focal attributes are important. Focal elements make it possible to give significant visual weight to specific visual lines or directions. These are of great help in directing movement, concentrating attention, or of distracting attention from minor and unpleasant part of the scene. With several focal elements, of varying attraction, it is possible to utilize several minor visual lines without destroying the most significant or upsetting the fundamental unity.

In utilizing bland landscapes, focal structures, color, or landscape elements will permit the generation of interesting and

stimulating elements, which may be able to subsitute reasonably
well for landscapes which are blessed with natural focal elements.

Enclosing

This term is used here to suggest the positive need for visual
limitation of functional areas. As a landscape needs subdivision
for functional purpose, so will it require visual expression of that
division.

Natural landscapes provide us with illustrative lessons in
plenty. Natural functions respond positively to variations in soil,
water, climatic variants, and abuse. The resulting visual forms are
satisfying expressions of these differences because it is possible
for the discerning to "read" their meaning and to understand why the
particular form which results is right and appropriate. It is not
unusual for natural conditions to generate responses which are consistent over definite areas and further, for such areas to have
distinct boundaries. By extension, looking at the character and
location of boundaries enables us to know much about the natural
conditions which produce them.

In like manner, the location and character of the boundaries
of made areas or functions enables us to know much about the function.
The extent of the boundary and its visual importance reveals something
of the functional importance. Its form and character are indicators
of both function and quality. As examples, the scale of a visible
clearing in wooded country can indicate the presence of a railroad,
a highway, or a powerline by differences in the size of the opening

and its location relative to the terrain. The materials used in a
fence help to describe the thing enclosed. The structure employed
along a shore boundary helps to describe the vessels which land,
the rise and fall of water, and the nature of storm conditions.

When boundary definition is made a major factor is permitting
the observer to understand the extent of functions which are taking
place in the water landscape, then it may be possible that made areas
and their boundaries will contain some of the same visual satisfactions as natural landscapes. If the design and character of enclosure is adequate, there will be a satisfying relationship expressed
between the functional requirement and the natural landscape which is
its setting.

Organizing

It is possible to evaluate the degree to which man-created
elements are capable of suggesting a functional organization. This
capability is important to avoid confusion misinterpretation, and
time-wasting which occurs when the visual appearance of a place is
inappropriate to its use. On the other hand, it is as bad that use
is expressed in a stark and blatant form which is in bleak contrast
to every other worthwhile visual value. A balance must be made between
the necessary functional expression and water landscape values.

Probably the simplest yet most important organizing attribute is
the proper indication of direction and location. Roads should suggest
both function and destination by whatever means are required. At
best, road location can be expressive of destination. Turnoffs are

made in the proper general direction. Landscape landmarks can be used to suggest a relationship between a junction and a destination. Distant views provide corraboration that one is indeed on the correct road. The visual quality of the road and its functional width and surface can reflect the quality of the destination. At the worst, proper signs can assist materially.

Evaluating the organizing characteristic should relate analysis of the sequence of events which is appropriate to a given functional use, with the visual clues provided to accomplish this. The sequence of approach, entrance, first visual impression, parking, getting information, accommodation, which is common to most water recreational functions suggests a sequence of visual requirements which is necessary to make the functional process work smoothly.

Examples of other organizing functions which may be evaluated are those which suggest the positional relationships between related elements, which suggest functional dominence or which simplify complex functional arrangements.

Modifying Enhancing

The evaluative term refers to those man-made structures, modifications, or treatments which are applied as a positive means for improving the visual quality of development. It is not used to describe possible changes to natural landscape, except when those changes are associated with development or structure.

Natural untrampled water and landscape needs no enhancement. Growth and decay, storm erosion, old age, and rebirth, are natural

causes of visual form which require no assistance from man to look
well. Only in the limited event that man's activities affect
natural process is indirect enhancement sometimes necessary or
desirable. For example, changes in water supply by dams upstream
may require that release flow be maintained in order that plant
communities continue. Fire hazard may require removal of some
hazardous material. Chemical protection from fire or for disease
treatment may be necessary.

This evaluation term applies to measures which may be applied
when natural conditions are altered by development and use. Most
construction requires that extensive measures be taken to safeguard
unaffected natural landscape, to repair traces of the work required,
and to design a fit between nature and structure which is satisfying
and appropriate.

Not all structure achieves the above objectives. Often erosion
caused by structural alteration to the landscape clogs streams and
muddies water clarity. Openings in a close forest cover leaves
new openings which are affected by wind and sunlight. Edges of
roads and clearings are left ragged and rubble filled. Roads and
clearings are formed without thought of fit or effect.

It is possible to modify, through proper design, the elements
we must build if we are to make adequate use of landscape and water.
Precautions can be taken to limit damaging changes. Drainage water
can be controlled, disturbed soil can be stabilized, and protection
given to permit an increase in traffic, water supply, and wear.

The forms of our structure and landscape can be such that there is unity of form: an absence of disruptive and uncontrolled contrast Such measures can be properly described as enhancing if they permit us to construct things necessary for human use, without serious disruption to the visual quality and continued good health of the surroundings.

LISTING OF COMPARATIVE AESTHETIC QUALITY FOR THE COMPONENTS OF THE
EVALUATIVE CLASSIFICATION: MAN-MADE ELEMENTS

Landscape Unit	Description of higher Quality	Description of lower Quality
Unifying	Access roads, trails passes, tunnels, and approaches are located to provide views which permit visual appraisal of the boundary and extent aspects of the setting unit.	Access roads and approaches located without consideration of need for traveler to understand form and extent of landscape
	Overlooks and viewpoints are located to permit view of boundary and extent in a more complete manner than is visible in a moving vehicle.	Few overlooks and viewpoints. Those available are limited to local features or roadside incidents.
	Linear, point and mass elements are concealed by location, reduced in contrast, and compliant in form so that the quality and character of the setting unit is unimpaired.	Many contrasting structures, point, and mass elements visible. No perceptible relationship between them. Detract from natural qualities by vividness competition.
	Clearings, scars, and linear edges are treated to reduce contrast and vividness. Objective: to avoid disrupting continuity of setting unit.	Scars, clearings and edges stand out as vivid areas of disruption to natural scene.
Focal	The most visually interesting, vivid, and spectacular elements are given acknowledgement in views, approaches, and accommodation. Provision of adequate view opportunities reduces erosive approaches.	Focal elements are poorly related to views and access. Often remote.

Focal (cont.)	Focal features are related to other aspects of setting unit. Features assist visual relationship to unit.	Features seen as isolated elements and attractions. Not ordinarily developed in relation to setting unit character.
	Structures, grading, and man-made focal features are de-emphasized, or concealed in views which help develop the setting unit boundary and extent.	Structures and man-made focal features are contrasty and vivid. Compete with important landscape features.
Enclosing	Overlooks, viewpoints and approaches develop views of bounding elements	Boundaries obscure or absent. Few opportunities to sight boundary elements. Internal circulation does not permit extensive views of enclosure of setting unit.
	Strongest, most vivid bounding elements are view preference.	Best views are of minor elements or minor boundaries.
Organizing	Roads, watercourses, rail lines, etc, where unavoidably visible may be aligned so that they assist in organizing, or giving form to bland and featureless units.	Unavoidably visible man-made features are unrelated to functional organization.
Enhancing	Displays of terrain models, maps and descriptive information permits more interesting and accurate interpretation of the visible elements.	Visitor must make his own interpretations. Displays limited to commerical inducements. No good maps.
	Modifications which subdue elements not in keeping with the quality and character of the setting unit. Ex.: Repair and reforestation of fire and windstorm, forest devastation; erosion prevention which affects visible stream color	Natural calamities which affect visual quality are unattended. Regulation and administration permit continuing practices which deteriorate natural quality.

Enhancing
(cont.)

and sedimentation; con-
cealment of isolated and
extraneous structures,
mining scars and dumps.

Planting or replanting
tree cover to assist
boundary definition, to
improve climate or com-
fort conditions, to aid
erosion, to provide
shelter for wildlife,
to replace forest har-
vest.

Planting haphazard or lacking
in purpose. Planting of
species which detract from
or provide sharp contrast to
natural materials.

Provision of comfortable
and readily visible free-
way turnoffs to scenic
settings, to provide
clear and adequate di-
rectional signs, to
publish up-to-date map
and directory informa-
tion.

Poorly visible junctions, few
directional signs, no maps or
directories of facilities
and accommodations available.

Avoid visual advertising
which generates abnor-
mal use and traffic be-
yond capacity of natural
area.

Visual advertising responsible
for degrading of setting unit
by overuse, crowding and wear.

Setting Unit	Higher Quality	Lower Quality
Unifying	Structures, facilities and functional improvements are designed to include all components in a related totality in which the whole is greater than the sum of the parts.	Facilities unplanned. Discontinuous design direction. Contrast of unharmonious elements, color form and material unsuitable; interactively destructive
	There is a visible and meaningful relationship between the visual forms and the evident function.	Structure or facility not related to functional form.
	Functional improvements are designed to complete and complement the landscape unit. If function is vividly antagonistic to natural quality, forms are subdued, function is made less contrasty and concealment is used where possible.	Improvements exhibit thoughtless siting and disregard for natural appearance and the unity of the landscape unit. Conspicuously degrading man-made elements or visible functional consequences such as smoke and pollution.
Focal	Necessary functional improvements are designed to evidence visual clarity of functional focus, and sense of destination.	Visually difficult to locate functional center. Destination unclear. Movement confusing.
	Best features of landscape and water are made visually available by development of views and provision for a variety of view angles.	No expression of the quality of landscape or water features. Little attempt to provide good visual outlook.
	In the absence of significant water focal features, structure and landscape are used positively to provide focal center of gravity.	Bland and featureless water landscapes are unrelieved by unifying focal center.

Focal (cont)	Natural focal water features are given primary positional advantage; structure and landscape avoid visual competition by position.	Existing natural features are degraded by nearby functional elements. Exploitation of natural elements.
Enclosing	Natural enclosing elements are utilized as fully as possible to complete sense of enclosure.	Location of structures and improvements not related to natural enclosure.
	Where natural elements are scarce, or absent, planting and grading are used as enclosure in preference to structure.	Needed enclosure formed by fences or other structure.
	Enclosing elements closely associated with water not disturbed in order to solve improvement problems.	Improvements are given primacy to the degree that water elements are adversely affected.
	Structural enclosure, where required, is not permitted to intrude visually.	Fences and screens are prominently visible and detrimental.
	Intensive human activities unrelated to the natural scene are enclosed and concealed (ex., parking).	Nodes of intense activity are highly visible.
Organizing	The functional aspects of the place are visually clear at first exposure. It is apparent where things are and little confusion about where to go.	Directions are usually necessary in order to find destination.
	"In" and "out" are clearly expressed. The end of the road or the last feature is expressed.	Visitors not sure how to get out or if they may have reached farthest extend of the development.

Organizing (cont.)	Secondary roads and trails are not confused with primary access.	Wasteful dead end and blind circulation common.
	Traffic flows are in orderly pattern.	Improper design and lack of direction creates traffic slowup and confusion.
	Buildings have primacy in both form and siting.	Buildings look alike. Signs or directions are necessary to locate activities.
	Functional zoning is practiced. Similar kinds of activity areas are related.	Noisy areas are disruptive of quiet activities.
Enhancing	The form and design of necessary improvements is not destructive of natural values.	Needed improvements have reduced natural quality by significant amount.
	Location of improvements make possible increased use of otherwise marginally scenic or compelling area.	Improvements do not consider desireable diffusion of intense use.
	Significant deterioration is arrested or controlled by suitable improvements.	Wear and deterioration are frequent and uncontrolled.
	Dead material, trash, and debris not visible competition with surroundings.	Trash and debris an eyesore.
	Green plants and turf maintained as a living addition to landscape to control surface conditions.	"Maintenance-free" paving and structure used as wearing surface.
	Characteristic land form is basis for topographic alteration.	Grading appears as vivid gouge in or flattening of contour.

Waterscape Unit	Higher Quality	Lower Quality
Unifying	The unity and integrity of the waterscape is pre-eminent.	Improvements visibly intrude on the unity and waterscape continuity.
	Stream or lacustrine bottom or shore improvements leave appearance unimpaired.	Improvements to bottom or shore are disunifying intrusion.
	The continuity and character of the hydrophytic and shore plants is a positive design factor.	Existing plant unity ignored or destroyed by substitution.
	No impediment to natural water supply or stable external management.	External water management produces sudden, seasonal, or emergency water supply variations which are visually unrelated to stream or receptacle.
Focal	The primary focus is along the stream or river or contained within broader lake, bay, or estuary boundaries.	Focus of attention is stimulated away from waterscape qualities.
	Secondary focal structures such as paths or access are closely related to stream focus.	Secondary focus developed between water and diverting element.
	Shore and access views take advantage of attractive distant views which provide linkage to setting and landscape units.	External views are unrelated to other units.
	Developmental foci are limited in favor of emphasizing water flow character, shore features, or streambed rocks.	Natural focal qualities are degraded by structural competition.

Enclosing	Natural enclosure related to water favored, protected and utilized.	Improvements and structures are more prominent enclosing agents.
	Enclosure which is a visible part of the setting or landscape unit emphasized to promote larger landscape continuity.	Relation to other stream areas or to the larger landscape is ignored.
	Shore planting protected and reinforced by maintenance of background planting.	Logging, agriculture, or urban development has seriously affected background planting.
	Upper and distant features of water enclosure are naturally undisturbed.	Mass and point elements such as excavations, spoil or power lines are part of background scene.
	When road or railroad construction forms part of the waterscape enclosure the form of the grading and its surface restoration are related to natural surroundings	Fills and embankments are raw and degrading realities.
	Shore water protection is designed to permit maximum water appearance potential and contact.	Shore protection forms isolating wall or limits access by height or slope.
Organizing	Improvements, structures and access promote basic shore or stream flow or character continuity.	Shore is seen as a succesion of places or structures; no real continuity.
	Access elements and circulation function as effective linkages to adjacent waterscape units and to the total water resource.	Access elements limited to isolated waterscape units.
	Shore drainage, intersecting streams, or outfalls are concealed, subdued, or treated in favor of waterscape continuity.	Shoreline is studded with pipes, outlets and other disruptive water input devices.

Enhancing (cont)	Drift, undermined trees and snags removed when their visual effect degrades waterscape unit.	Waterscape unit visual quality and water flow adversely affected by drift accumulations and fallen trees.
	Shore drainage erosion and damage to shorelines controlled.	Stream or lake badly affected by runoff damage caused by shore water entering waterscape unit.
	When the water area is encumbered by excessive plant growth, some removal may restore.	Evident deterioration of waterscape continuity by unchecked and untended plant growth.
	Replanting to restore flood damage, logging, or high use damage.	No planting in damaged or harvested areas. These conditions permit weedy or foreign new growth.

SECTION IV

RECOMMENDATIONS

Concerning the Aesthetic Role of Water in the Landscape

These recommendations represent a summary of the principal
concepts and directions indicated by the foregoing text. They are
grouped under three broad areas, each with subdivisions:

A.   GENERAL POLICY ADOPTION

     An Aesthetic Appraisal Policy

     A Design Guideline Policy

B.   PLANNING GUIDELINES FOR AESTHETICS IN THE WATER LANDSCAPE

     Evaluations and Selection

     Planning for Unity and Variety

     Administration, Management

C.   RESEARCH NEEDS

     Benefit Comparisons

     Design Studies

     Behavioral Relationships and Observer Response

     Computer Application

A.   GENERAL POLICY ADOPTION

An Aesthetic Appraisal Policy

A specific policy concerned with the aesthetic and environmental role of water in the landscape needs common adoption across
the lines of Federal agencies that affect water resources. The
National Environmental Policy Act of 1969 does pose the generalities of responsibility for "esthetically pleasing environments
and evaluation of "environmental amenities." But generalities are
insufficient guidance to an esoteric problem. Federal agencies
vary so much in their capacity to address aesthetic problems that
their various interpretations of the National Environmental Policy
Act must be considered difficult to coordinate and unify. Thus
there is the need for one specific definitive aesthetic policy for
use in appraisal of native conditions and of developmental impacts.

It is suggested that there is urgent need to adopt an interim
policy in order that further erosion of existant aesthetic qualities
be avoided. In the absence of other tools of visual inventory and
evaluation, it is respectfully suggested that the classification
framework and associated elements of this report as refined by a
selected panel of experts working with the Council on Environmental
Quality, be considered as a starting point. (See Research Needs).

A Design Guideline Policy

There is need also for general adoption of forward looking design guidelines that are more sympathetic and compatible with water

related modifications that certain of those now being used by individual agencies. Adoption of a unified policy on design guidelines would set broad standards of performance, giving better coordination among agencies. This would not be a substitute for
the detailed managerial design guidelines necessary for individual
agencies.

A panel of experienced and capable individuals, selected
from various and other private/public situations as well, should
be engaged to proceed with development of such guidelines. The
design perspective within this report is suggested for introductory
use to this purpose.

B. PLANNING GUIDELINES FOR AESTHETICS IN THE WATER LANDSCAPE

Evaluations and Selection

Evaluations and selection of water landscapes should be con-
ducted in reference to:

Physiographic regions and provinces of the United States
(possibly North America) or major drainage systems or basins (i.e.
Missouri drainage). Within each of these regions there should be
at least one representative of each of the three water landscape
designations: wild, scenic, and recreational.

Administrative level of government relevant to the significi-
cance of public interest; water landscapes that are considered to
be of national significance would be identified by a Federal evaluation within the entire country. Each State should determine the
relative quality of water landscapes within their jurisdiction.
Each regional or county government could select those water landscapes that would have local significance (possibly as a component
of open space or recreation planning program).

● Accessibility to both present and future users: concentric zones that describe travel time from a population should relate the amount and quality of water landscapes to their capability to provide users with experiences of aesthetic merit. Usually water landscapes near urban areas may have a lower level of aesthetic quality than remote streams and lakes. However, because of **accessibility**, the lower aesthetic qualities can have a high value to the public-at-large. The more accessible the water body is to user concentrations, the greater should be the value placed on protecting or improving its aesthetic qualities.

● All water landscapes, no matter how degraded by human impacts, should be considered to have an inherent aesthetic value (assuming all will eventually have pollution abatement and control).

The aesthetic values (either real or potential) of developed, urban, or degraded water landscapes are as worthy of protection and improvement as the well publicized values of wild and scenic rivers. To a significant number of viewers the aesthetic value of a developed river could be as great as a wild river. Evaluation should consider the potentiality of all water landscapes to provide a variety of aesthetic experiences.

● Water landscapes that have been degraded in aesthetic quality by developmental impacts should be rehabilitated to provide more opportunity to satisfy a range of aesthetic preferences and thereby relieve pressure on the limited number of high quality

water landscapes. The fact that water landscapes do have inherent aesthetic value does not mean that the addition of water
to non-water landscape will increase the level of aesthetic
quality. Water may inundate a landscape of higher aesthetic
quality than it creates (i.e. Glen Canyon and Lake Powell).

● The evaluation of water landscapes at the regional level
(Landscape Units) should recognize the unity developed by the
combined appearance of all the region's water bodies.

All water bodies of a region -- whether fluvial or lacustrine -- contribute to a common experience of water. The distinction between fluvial and lacustrine expressions tends to
blend into one regional comprehension of water. However, Federal
and state programs have been directed at protecting the fluvial
bodies of a region, and comparatively little regard has been
given to protection of lacustrine bodies. There is limited
Federal and state concern for the protection of lakes comparable
to the interest demonstrated by the wild and scenic rivers programs. The aesthetic values of lacustrine landscapes in some
regions can be as great or greater than that of adjacent wild
or scenic rivers -- yet, they are not offered the same protection
against adverse aesthetic impact as are fluvial bodies.

● Evaluation of water landscapes in terms of recreational
use (such as use days) does not reflect the aesthetic qualities
of the area:

The recreation benefit procedures presently used by Federal
agencies such as the Corps of Engineers and the Bureau of Reclamation are based on the underlying premise that the greater
the use, the greater the recreational value. However, the
aesthetic values of the recreation experience will likely decrease in quality with increased numbers of users. In terms of
aesthetic quality, it would be more nearly valid to estimate
the recreational benefit on a day use value that decreases with
increased daily attendance at the water landscape.

Planning for Unity and Variety

● Planning should recognize both the unity inherent in a
water setting and the continuity it possesses along its length.

Water bodies are defined by the settings that contain them.
The water and the enclosing setting should be considered as a
mutually reinforcing unit. Water that expresses itself as a
continuous element, such as a river or a large lake system,
should be considered as a continuum of experience along its
course. Evaluations should not be made on isolated segments as
if they had no connection to the total water body.

● In urban areas, water bodies should be treated as a continuous element that will serve to strongly define and interconnect
an open space system. Development should reinforce and not
break the unity and continuity of the natural drainage system.

● Water landscapes should be planned and managed to the limits of the Setting Unit:

Visual protection of water body depends on control of the setting landscape, not just the waterscape. The aesthetic values of the water body are to a large degree dependent on the quality of the setting within which the water body lies.

● Environmental control zones such as recommended by the Bureau of Reclamation should be established on those areas of the setting unit that are highly sensitive to visual disturbance (visual vulnerability;* Lake Tahoe Regional Plan). Lands in high vulnerability zones should remain or be restored to their natural state. The use of scenic easements may accomplish the desired protection of setting quality without necessitation outright acquisition.

● Evaluation should recognize the variety that naturally exists along a water landscape:

Guidelines for the development along the water landscape should be based on the awareness of diversity and should be designed to bring out fully the potentially unique experience inherent in each part of the water landscape. Developments along a water landscape should not decrease the diversity of contrast among setting units and waterscape units. (If a river is to be impounded at several locations, intervals between dams need to be long enough to allow free flowing water contrast).

● Planning should recognize the variety that naturally exists among water landscapes:

---

*Visual vulnerability:relative capacity of a native landscape to accept change without showing conspicuous disturbance.

The diversity that exists in water landscapes (urban water-fronts, wild rivers, pastoral streams, recreational impoundments) should be maintained to reflect the evident pluralism of the user demands and satisfactions.

● A significant proportion of the population may prefer a well designed urban waterscape to wild river experience. Neither preservation nor development of water landscapes should significantly decrease the diversity of aesthetic opportunities in the region. A breadth of opportunities should be provided so that the preferences of all observer groups could -- to varying degrees -- be accommodated. Preferences of users for a type of aesthetic environment could be expanded by informational programs to conform with a complete variety of water landscapes rather than concentrating on one or two types of water landscapes (i.e. wild rivers). Since it is apt to be physically impossible to meet increasing demands for wilderness experience, reorientation to the opportunities of other kinds of water landscapes through education may be possible.

● The aesthetic qualities of the water landscape must be considered at the preplanning stage of the project, as well as the subsequent stages of development:

Traditionally, aesthetic concerns have been included in the project program at the final stages of design to "beautify" or cosmetically "improve" the physical impact. This is too late.

● If the project has locational flexibility, a comparative analysis could be made of the respective aesthetic qualities of each of the possible sites. The comparative analysis could be based on the classification system proposed by this report. The project should be sited on the water landscape location where the least amount of cumulative aesthetic values would be foregone by development. If the project has no locational flexibility, or once the site of least aesthetic values has been determined, a further, more intensive aesthetic analysis should be made of the specific location. The analysis should develop siting and design guidelines that would, at the very least, minimize or ameliorate the adverse visual impact of the project. Preferably, the need to be compatible with the particular aesthetic qualities of the water landscape location should be stressed.

● Planning and design of a whole project, including aesthetic concerns, is logically the effort of an interdisciplinary team. While the composition of teams will vary from project to project, it is essential that there be control from the outset by the goals established for and by the team. The best possible designers need to be a part of such a team.

● The building of new water landscapes, starting with deteriorated or mediocre setting units, suggests a bold way of relieving excessive use pressures upon superior natural units. This procedure could also provide advantages of location and access not necessarily associated with a natural unit.

● The protection of either the outstanding or typical characteristics of a setting unit must presume a limitation upon the
amount of facilities and use that can be allowed in a specific
situation. The qualities of a unit which invite its use must
be conserved so that development does not become over-development
with consequent degradation of the whole.

Administration, Management

● Agencies should be encouraged to examine the aesthetic impacts normally associated with their operations and past projects
as an ongoing research program:

Siting and design criteria should be developed for all
facilities or operations they normally place in the water landscape.
To some degree this has already been accomplished with the Bureau
of Reclamation's Circular 376 - Environmental Quality Preservation
and Enhancement. New criteria should be developed as observer's
reaction to specific aesthetic impacts either change or are further
made known.

● New techniques of engineering, construction, or operation
should be continually investigated for the improved appearance
advantages they may offer over existing methods. Characteristics
of projects which are particularly compatible with their use and
environment should be documented for incorporation into future
work.

C. RESEARCH NEEDS

Benefit Comparisons

●   Determine the merits of incorporating the benefits foregone approach in cost-benefit analysis:

Should the agency proposing development be required to cite
the benefits foregone as well as the benefits to be derived from
developing a water landscape? Should user day value figures be
revised to reflect the difference in aesthetic experience of
different water landscapes? Supportive research is necessary
to determine if there are higher aesthetic values people would
be willing to pay for in wild river situations than on impounded
rivers -- therefore higher value of benefits foregone.

●   Investigation should be made of the validity of ascribing
the same user day value to all water landscapes, particularly
the value of a user day on a river before impoundment being
equivalent to the value of a user day after impoundment.

●   Determine the merits of the proposition that benefits of a
development in a water landscape will, at best, increase at
slower rate than the benefits accruing from preserving a rare
pristine water landscape (of which there is a fixed supply).

Will the benefits of rare, irreplacable natural assets in
fixed supply appreciate with time, other things being equal?
Is it possible to predict the different rates of appreciation
and would the rates be differentiated to reflect relative
aesthetic qualities of the supply?

Determine how the aesthetic values of water landscapes can be related to the economic concepts of a safe minimum standard and of option demand:

How will increasing pressures for developing water landscapes effect the ability to preserve future alternative opportunities for aesthetic experience? Should a number and type of water landscape be preserved to insure at least one full range of aesthetic opportunity? Is it possible to determine for any water landscape, through sampling, the approximate number of all people who value the preservation at the level of existing aesthetic qualities? The sample should include those people who have not visited the site but find pleasure in knowing that the water landscape retains its aesthetic quality. To what extent is it possible to measure the value this total number would place or be willing to pay for retention of the aesthetic qualities?

Design Studies

A system of defining and evaluating water dominated or oriented environments is needed in which aesthetic criteria are primary tools. This relates directly to Sec. 102(B) of the National Environmental Policy Act (Public Law 91-190). The Council on Environmental Quality should sponsor and support such design research (Sec. 204(5)).

Design studies of past projects need to be undertaken for the identification of successful or failing elements and relationships both within developments and their linkage to landscape. Scrutiny of individual case studies as well as comparison among cases should reveal strong or weak points, areas of overuse or marginal use. Evolution of new and superior development patterns of design for application to future work could result.

● Hypothetical identification of elements and relationships found in the landscape and in development need to be subjected to psychological and sociological appraisal. Planning and design criteria may be improved through preference testing and conformity or disconformity with general opinion examination. Yet mere popularity should not be allowed to cancel the potential values and richness that can come from design.

● Team work research among designers and psychologists and sociologists suggests a fertile field for the improvement of planning and design procedures. It is a form of investigation concerned with the environment which is only now beginning.

Behavioral Relationships and Observer Response

● A number of interesting research questions pertain to the area of water-landscape aesthetics, the answers to which would be of immediate and direct value to water resource planners and managers. They fall conveniently into three classes: 1) determining those qualities or attributes of water landscapes which are of universal aesthetic appeal, i.e., which increase aesthetic satisfaction; 2) determining those aspects of water landscapes which are universally (or generally) disliked, ie.e., the factors which decrease aesthetic satisfaction or appeal; 3) determining - and finding the significant personal correlates of - those factors which are differently valued by different people, i.e., those which some people like and others dislike. Answers to the first two questions will yield data which will serve as basic aesthetic operating principles for planners and managers for any water resource, regardless of intended use or likely observer groups. The third question - falling well within the domain of the psychology of individual differences - will be useful in any situation in which the planner or manager anticipates and wishes to take into account the diverging aesthetic preferences of various user, observer, or other special interest groups. (See the Appendix for a more detailed description of behavior research directions.)

Computer Application

● The visual complexity within and among water landscapes suggests the application of computer technology in order to free the decision maker from the tedious and mechanical tasks of analysis and display of his conceptualizations. The usefulness of the results will necessarily reflect the logic and validity of the basic data provided.

● Any continuous, real or spatial data (i.e. vegetation, water surface, etc) can be quantified, inventoried, stored, retrieved, and spatially displayed using x-y coordinate systems.

● Relational measures of dimension (i.e. height, width, depth, and volume) express enclosure and can be machine computed and displayed statistically (e.g., an index of setting enclosure can be developed through explicit condition statements relating dimensions) and graphically (e.g., providing machine driven plots of the unit -- sections, elevations, plan views, isometric and perspective views, etc.).

● Topographic data (elevation) as a single data item can be utilized to compute slope and aspect (TOPOGO) and visibility (VIEWIT), as well as computer driven plots (DRAW), perspectives, isometrics (SYMVU), and shaded grid maps (GRID). This suggests that elevation alone can serve to compute and map a number of visual indices at a coarse grain of analysis. With the addition of vegetation type and density plus water type, available through aerial photo interpretation, a reasonably fine-grained analysis is possible. By including supplementary field data recording specific features such as waterfalls, cataracts, cascades, gorges, rock outcroppings, and pinnacles, a high degree of visual resolution can be achieved. This flexibility in scale is a major advantage of the computer, since once data is stored it can be retrieved and displayed at virtually any desired scale.

● Through a process of cell differentiation and pattern recognition, objectified relational measures can be computed for visual units. Explicit criterion, in the form of condition statements, can be developed to measure unity, variety and vividness within and among units. In addition, measures of "difference" can be determined for any desired measure of visual organization (i.e., prominence, pattern, contrast, uniqueness, diversity, continuity, feature isolation, transition). Light conditions and seasonal variations can be included, providing a dynamic mode to the analysis, and combinations of these measures can express significant visual aspects of water landscape characteristics.

APPENDIX A

APPENDIX A

Terms Descriptive of Water Landscapes

Fluvial Types

Bayou
Braided stream
Brook
Canal
Connecting stream
Creek
Disappearing stream
Feeder stream
Fluvial lakes
Freshet
Inlet
Influent
Intermittent stream
Interrupted stream
Misfit river
Outlet
Raft
Rill
River
Slough
Spring
Stream
Torrent
Vigorously meandering
    stream
Watercourse
Waterway

Lacustrine Types

Aestival ponds
Alkali lakes
Alluvial dam lakes
Alpine lakes
Bar lake
Barrier lake
Bayou
Blind lake
Blowout pond
Bog lake
Borrow pit pond
Caldera lake
Chain of lakes

Charco
Cirque lake
Clear lake
Closed lake
Crater lake
Dead lake
Deflation lake
Delta lake
Doline lake
Drainage lake
Dry lake
Dugout pond
Dune lake
Dystrophic lake
Effluent lake
Evanescent lake
Extinct lake
Farm pond
Finger lake
Fission lake
Fluvial lake
Fluviatile lake
Fosse lake
Glacial lake
Grass lake
Headwaters lake
Holding pond
Holm lake
Hot springs
Impoundment
Intermittent lake
Kettle lake
Lagoon
Lake
Lakelet
Landslide lake
Laguna
Lateral lake
Marl lake
Marsh lake
Meadow lake
Mesotrophic lake
Mill pond
Mirror lake
Moat lake

Morainal lake
Nova lake
Oligotrophic lake
Open lake
Oriented lake
Oxbow
Palodolac
Perched lake
Perennial lake
Pit lake
Playa
Pond
Pool
Pothole
Puddle
Quarry pond
Raft lake
Reflection basin
Rejuvenated lake
Reservoir
Ria lakes
Rift lakes
Riverine lakes
Rock lakes
Sag pond
Salt lakes
Satellite lakes
Scour lakes
Seepage lakes
Senescent lake
Sink lakes
Slough
Snag lake
Strath lake
Swarm of lakes
Tailing pond
Tanks
Tarn
Thaw lakes
Tundra lakes
Vernal & autumnal ponds
Walled lakes

Water Features and Patterns

(F - usually associated with fluvial expressions)
(L - usually associated with lacustrine expressions)

Antidune (F)	Mouth
Arm (L)	Narrows
Backwater	Neck cutoff (F)
Bay (L)	Neckfluve (L)
Bay head (L)	Outlet (L)
Bayou	Pass
Bend (F)	Passage
Boil (F)	Plunge pool (F)
Braids (F)	Pool (F)
Branch (F)	Pothole (F)
Cascade (F)	Rapid (F)
Cataract (F)	Reach
Channel	Riffle (F)
Chute	Rift (F)
Cove (L)	Ripple
Cutoff (F)	Rollers (F)
Deadwater (F)	Scour pools (F)
Debouchure (F)	Shallows
Disciplined waters (F)	Shooting water (F)
Eddy (F)	Sinuous channel (F)
Entrenched meander (F)	Slack water
Fork (F)	Slough
Free meander (F)	Sound (L)
Geysers	Standing water
Goosenecks (F)	Straight channel (F)
Gut (L)	Strait
Harbor	Streaming water (F)
Headwaters	Swirls
Inclosed meanders (F)	Torrent (F)
Inlet (L)	Waterfalls - Falls (F)
Lagoon	Waves (L)
Meander (F)	White Water (F)
	Wind streaks

Water Related Landforms and Vegetative Conditions

(F - usually associated with fluvial expressions)
(L- usually associated with lacustrine expressions)

Abandoned channel
Alluvial terrace (F)
Arroyo (F)
Bank
Bar
Basin (L)
Beach
Beds - bed material
Bluff
Bog
Braid bar (F)
Canyon (F)
Cape
Channel mouth bar (F)
Chasm (F)
Chimney
Cliff
Cut bank (F)
Delta (F)
Drawdown rim (L)
Dunes (F)
False shoreline (L)
Flood plain
Flood plain outwash (F)
Flume (F)
Ford (F)
Gap (F)
Gorge (F)
Gulch (F)
Gully (F)
Head
Island - Isle
Knickpoint (F)
Lacustrine plain (L)
Ledge
Lenticular island and bar (F)
Lobe (F)
Marsh
Meadow
Meander scar (F)
Morass
Mud flat
Narrows
Natural bridge

Natural levee (F)
Neck
Notch (F)
Open shore (L)
Overbank deposits (F)
Paired terraces (F)
Palisades
Peninsula
Point bar (F)
Point
Portage
Presque isle
Promontory
Puddin' bed (L)
Quagmire
Quondam island
Rand (L)
Ravine (F)
Recession flats (L)
River-cut plain (F)
River flat (F)
Sand ribbon (F)
Scarp
Scour depressions (F)
Shoal
Spit (L)
Spur
Stack
Stream terrace (F)
Stream flutes (F)
Swale
Swamp
Tongue (F)
Tombolo (L)
Trench (F)
Treshold (L)
Trough
Valley plug (F)
Wash (F)
Water gap (F)

References:

Allen, R.L., Current Ripples, 1968.

Moore, W.G., Dictionary of Geography, 1967.

American Geological Institute, Dictionary of Geologic Terms, 1960.

Morisawa, Marie, Streams: Their Dynamics and Mythology, 1968.

Veatch, J.O. and Humphrys, C.R., Water and Water Use Terminology, 1966.

Additional References:

Chow, Ven Te, Open Channel Hydraulics, 1959.

Leopold, L.B. and Maddock,   The Hydraulic Geometry of Stream
    Channels and Some Physiographic Implications, USGS Paper 252, 1953.

Leopold, L.B. and Wolman, G.M., Fluvial Processes in Geomorphology, 1964.

Leopold, L.B. and Wolman, G.M., "River Channel Patterns: Braided,
    Meandering, and Straight", USGS Prof. Paper 282B, 1957.

Leopold, L.B. and Wolman, G.M., "River Meanders", Geological Society
    of American Bulletin, V. 71, pp. 769-794, June 1960.

Matthes, G.H., "Macroturbulence in Natural Stream Flow", Transactions-
    American Geophysical Union, Vol. 28, No. 2, pp. 255-261.

Maxson, J.H. and Campbell, I., "Stream Fluting and Stream Erosion",
    Journal of Geology, Vol. 43, No. 7, pp. 729-744, 1935.

Schummn, S.A., "Sinuosity of the Alluvial Rivers of the Great Plains",
    Geological Society of America Bulletin, Vol. 74, pp. 1089-1100,
    July-Dec. 1963.

Thomas, H.E., "Cultural Control of Water Development", Ciba Journal,
    pp. 25-32, Autumn 1964.

Werner, R.W., "On the Origin of River Meanders", Transactions-American
    Geophysical Union, Vol. 32, pp. 898-902, 1951.

Wolman, G.M. and Leopold, L.B., "River Flood Plains: Some Observations
    on Their Formation", USGS Prof. Paper 282-C 1957.

APPENDIX B

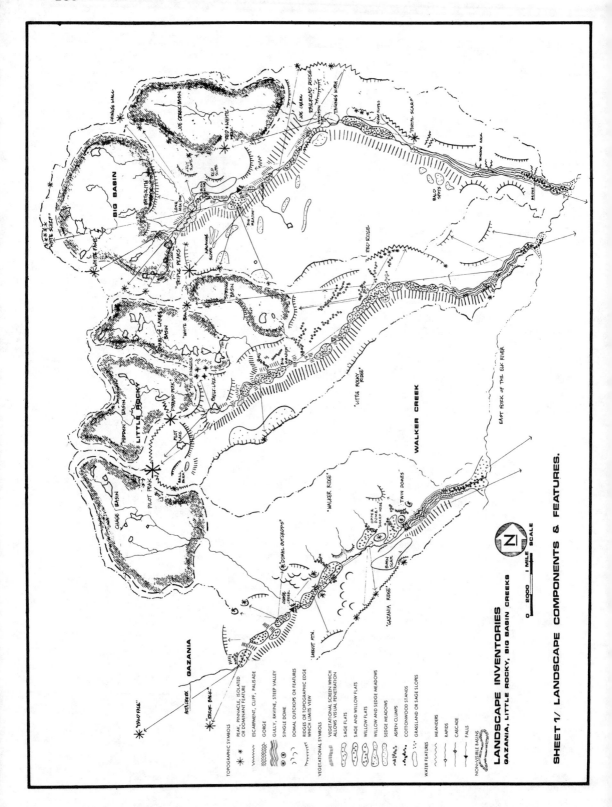

LANDSCAPE INVENTORIES
GAZANIA, LITTLE ROCKY, BIG BASIN CREEKS

SHEET 1/ LANDSCAPE COMPONENTS & FEATURES.

TOPOGRAPHIC SYMBOLS

- PEAK, PINNACLE, ISOLATED OR DOMINANT FEATURE
- ESCARPMENT, CLIFF, PALISADE
- GORGE
- GULLY, RAVINE, STEEP VALLEY
- SINGLE DOME
- DOMAL OUTCROPS OR FEATURES
- RIDGES OR TOPOGRAPHIC EDGE WHICH LIMITS VIEW

VEGETATIONAL SYMBOLS

- VEGETATIONAL SCREEN WHICH ALLOWS VISUAL PENETRATION
- SAGE FLATS
- SAGE AND WILLOW FLATS
- WILLOW FLATS
- WILLOW AND SEDGE MEADOWS
- SEDGE MEADOWS
- ASPEN CLUMPS
- COTTONWOOD STANDS
- GRASSLAND OR SAGE SLOPES

WATER FEATURES

- MEANDERS
- RAPIDS
- CASCADE
- FALLS

NON-VISIBLE BASINS

SCALE
0   2000   1 MILE

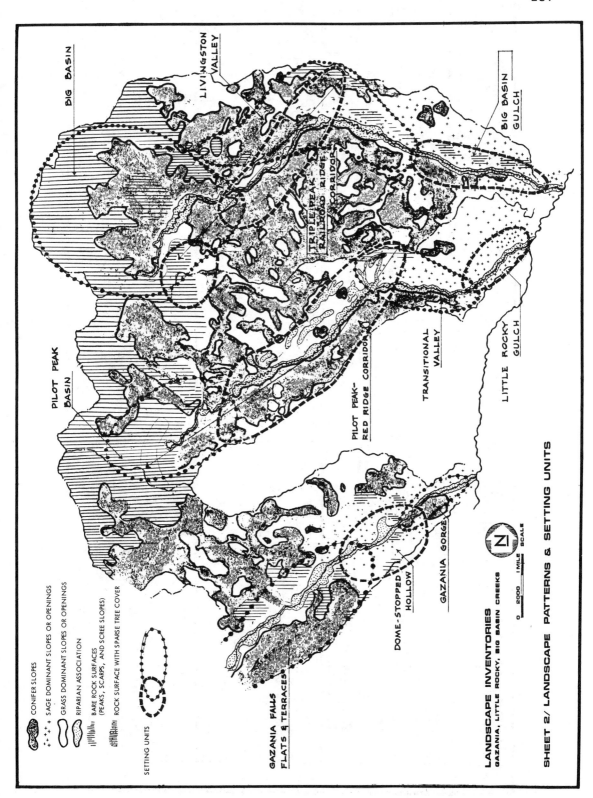

LIVINGSTON VALLEY

BIG BASIN

BIG BASIN GULCH

TRIPLE PEAK – RAILROAD RIDGE

PILOT PEAK BASIN

PILOT PEAK – RED RIDGE RIDGE CORRIDOR

TRANSITIONAL VALLEY

LITTLE ROCKY GULCH

GAZANIA GORGE

DOME-STOPPED HOLLOW

GAZANIA FALLS FLATS & TERRACES

CONIFER SLOPES

+ + + + + SAGE DOMINANT SLOPES OR OPENINGS

GRASS DOMINANT SLOPES OR OPENINGS

RIPARIAN ASSOCIATION

BARE ROCK SURFACES (PEAKS, SCARPS, AND SCREE SLOPES)

ROCK SURFACE WITH SPARSE TREE COVER

SETTING UNITS

LANDSCAPE INVENTORIES
GAZANIA, LITTLE ROCKY, BIG BASIN CREEKS

N

0   2000   1 MILE
SCALE

SHEET 2/ LANDSCAPE PATTERNS & SETTING UNITS

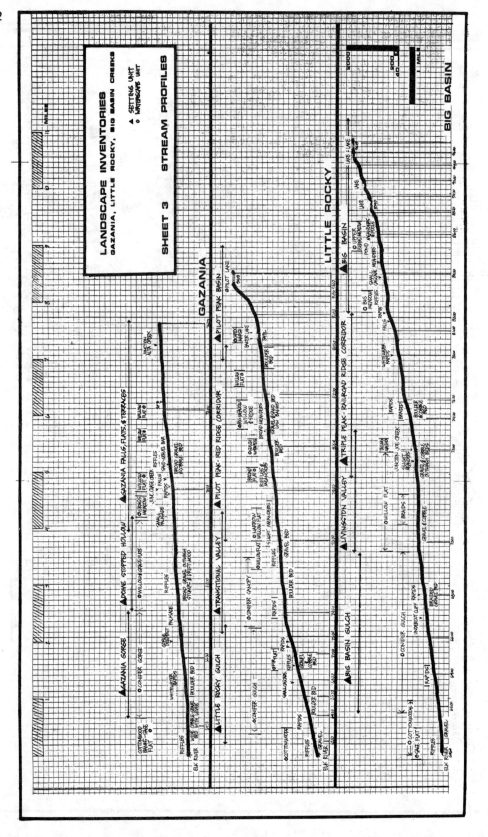

APPENDIX C

APPENDIX C

The Factors Selected by various Investigators
as a Basis for Aesthetic Quality Evaluations

California Department of Water Resources
"Guidelines for the Evaluation of General Recreation"

Factors to be considered in determining the esthetic qualities
in the site:

Fluctuations of water surface
Geologic-topographic (unique, colorful, large, significant,
    precious, varied, durable)
Vegetative cover (unique, beautiful, perennial, well located,
    durable, shade, large)
Climate (temperature extremes, storms, long recreation season,
    predictable weather)
Aquatic characteristics (large or extensive, clean and pure,
    attractive and safe)
Other environmental influences (opportunity for seclusion,
    distractions from unrelated activity, noise, odor, unsightly
    works, absence of unsightly major transportation routes, pests)

California Resources Agency
California Protected Waterways Plan

Scenic Quality:

River sections rated independently as follows:
AAA - outstanding, one of the most scenic and unspoiled of
      California rivers
AA - Very beautiful
A   - Beautiful, scenic
B   - Average scenery, a pleasant run
C   - Below average, uninteresting run from scenic standpoint
D   - Poor, low scenic values or significant lengths marred
      by man's activities

It is clear, though, that a portion of a waterway's intrinsic scenic
value lies in the contiguous lands.

285

Dearinger, J.A.
Esthetic and Recreational Potential of Small Naturalistic Streams

Value rating of scenery:

    Occurance and quality of geologic values
    Percent of total watershed in forest
    Percent of total watershed in land use capability classes VI,
        VII, VIII
    Percent of stream length in certain stream order category
    Occurance and quality of land husbandry value

Leopold, L.B.
"Quantitative Comparison of Some Aesthetic Factors Among Rivers"

    Field evaluation of aesthetic factors:
    Physical factors   Human Use and Interest
        River width at low flow   Number of occurences
        Depth at low flow   of trash and litter
        Velocity at low flow   Material removable
        Bankful depth   Artificial controls
        Flow variability   Accessability
        River pattern   Individual
        Ratio of valley height to width   Mass Use
        Bed material   Local Scene
        Bed slope   Vistas
        Basin area   View confinement
        Stream order   Land use
        Erosion of banks   Utilities
        Deposition   Degree of change
                                                  Recovery potential
    Biologic and water quality factors   Urbanization
        Water color   Special views
        Turbidity   Historic features
        Floating material   Misfits
        Water condition
        Algae
        Larger plants
        River -auna
        Pollution evidence
        Land flora
          Valley
          Hillslope
          Diversity
          Condition

Comparisons for groups factors selected to represent particular aspects of the landscapes:

Landscape scale = width or valley related to height of nearby hills
Landscape interest = landscape scale related to scenic outlook
Scale of valley character = landscape interest related to urbanization
Measure of river size = river depth related to river width
Scale of river character = measure of river size to prevalance of rapids

Morisawa, M. and Murie, M.
Evaluation of Natural Rivers

Aesthetic factors:

Landscape
    views and vistas
    diversity of flora and geologic features
    color
    form and contrasts
Sensual stimuli
    temperature regime
    winds and other aerial features
    sounds
    odors
    visual patterns
Intellectual interests
    opportunities for interpretive programs
    ecology
    geology
    wildlife
    range and diversity of subjects available for study
Emotional interest
    physical stimuli
    intellectual potentials
    possibility for adventure
    interaction of flora, fauna, and people
    access
    climatic factors
Obstacles or discomforts
    troublesome flora and fauna
    access
    climatic factors
Culture
    quality of land use management construction
    scenic pollution
    historic artifacts

Subjective analysis of most important factors
in viewing river - most significant in deriving
pleasurable feelings:
   vista
   color
   vegetation (amount and variety)
   spaciousness
   serenity
   naturalness
   riffles in water
   turbidity
   lack of pollution

Nighswonger, J.J.
A Methodology for Inventorying and Evaluating the Scenic Quality
and Related Recreational Value of Kansas Streams

   Criteria for Study Area Consideration:

      Water-quantity and flow rate (including seasonal variation)
      Topographic change - contrasting relief, welcome variety,
         scenic view points
      Forest vegetation - visual variety and contrast, stream bank
         and soil stabilization, climate control, seasonal color
         variation

   Recreational Resource Inventory
      (Resource rated according to contribution to: 1) visual
      quality and 2) recreational usability)

Resources:	Categorized by:
Access	ease or difficulty of access
Riffles	maneuverability and floatability
Rapids	maneuverability and floatability
Waterfall	vertical drop(s)
Dam	navigability and water flows
Bluff	rock outcrops, vertical faces, strongly sloping
Spring	origin at stream or tributary
Bridge	navigability, vehicular traffic, non-vehicular use
Natural campsite	stream and road access, attractive and suitable site
Improved campsite	extent of facilities provided
Specimen plant	unique-growth pattern or character, size, presence

Cave   Not categorized, only presence
                                      recorded
Pipe line
Scenic site
Historic site
Rock and fossil area
Wetlands
Scenic vista

Detriments to Recreational Quality:
Bank pollution
Water pollution

Research Planning and Design Associates, Inc.
The Susquehanna River Watershed: The Impact of Water on the Visual
Landscape

   Visual analysis criteria when introducing water into the landscape:
      Setting
         relation of horizontal plane of water to verticals topo sides
         number and types of vantage points
         area of water surface visible from single point
         kinds of land uses and intensities that can occur around
            water bodies (percent slope)
      Nature of water (streams, lakes, waterfalls)
      Intensity of experience (experiencing water in time along a route)
      Water surface elevation (creative tool for determining interesting
         shorelines)

Tennessee Department of Conservation
Tennessee's Scenic Rivers

   Evaluation Criteria:

      Year around stream flow
      Natural features (scenic ecological, and geological features)
      Access to Stream (ranked by river class)
      Water quality (pollution, temperature, turbidity, etc.)
      Stream bank conditions (revegetation necessity, degree of
         disturbance)
      Historical data (written and verbal reports)
      Archeological data (known sites)

U.S. Bureau of Outdoor Recreation - Northeast Region
An Environmental Quality Rating System

    Water Resources - 60 points (Water resources one of six categories
       that compose the rating system)

       Unique waterway - 3 (contribution to visual variety)
       Distinctive water forms - 5 (significance and representative
         forms found throughout area)
       Water resource stability - 6 (in balance with natural order)
       Water surface ratio - 6 (area water surface more than 2% and
         less than 10% of gross acers)
       Lakes and ponds - 10 (varying sizes and shapes, well distributed -
         few, small difficult access)
       Streams - 10 (many, well distributed, varying in quality and
         perennial - few, intermittant)
       Salt water - 10 (varying to uniform shoreline)
       Rivers - 10 (based on size)

U.S. Federal Water Pollution Control Administration
Report of the Committee on Water Quality Criteria

    Recommended criteria for aesthetic purposes:
      All surface waters contribute to support of life forms of
        aesthetic value
      Surface waters free of substances attributable to discharges
        or waste
      Waters of unique or special interest by reason of clarity,
        scenic setting, or other characteristics

Whitman, I.L.
Uses of Small Urban River Valleys

Environmental Factors:	Characteristics:
Water quality	Quality characteristic perceptible without formal analysis
Vegetation	High degree of land covered by vegetation, species diversity
Habitat	Presence of fish, mammals, birds, butterflies, absence of pests
Valley view from above	Impact of panoramic view over the whole valley
Valley view from below	Minimum view of outside development, view of trees on hillcrests
Flood plain vista	Absence of sturctures, etc. in longitudinal view along flood plain
Channel appearance	Naturalistic banks and beds, freedom from encroaching structures

APPENDIX D

APPENDIX D

Further Research of Observer Response to Water Landscapes

For the purpose of research direction, the observer response to water landscapes can be conveniently divided into three classes:

1. Universally Valued Water Qualities

The planner-manager undoubtedly harbors a rich and diverse set of hypotheses about the qualities of water that contribute to a positive aesthetic experience, i.e., that people in general like or find pleasing. Many of these are based on intuition or common sense, and must be subjected to empirical analysis.

A catalog of these qualities follow:

Non-Visible Qualities

Sound

Smell

Touch (heat, cool, fluid)

Balance (buoyancy)

Taste - thirst

Known Potential for a Recreational Pleasure:

Fishing, Seimming, Boating, Sailing, Scuba, Canoeing, Water Skiing, Rowing, Contemplation, Photography, Painting, Wildlife Watching, Collecting, etc.

Visible Qualities

Movement (gravity movement, wind movement, mechanical,

fountain)

Placidity

Transparency

Reflection - mirror sparkling light - water as a modifier

of light

Color

Space-Openness-Distance-Space in enclosed areas

Enclosure-Boundary-Limit-Containment

Plain Surface-Horizontal Sheet

Inclined and Vertical Surface

Unity of Element-Continuity of Direction, Linking

Element - Orientation

Landscape Focus (lowest point in landscape) - Orientation

Water Landscapes have Balance - Symmetry to Shore

Definitions

Contrast to Land (less seen than land) - Relative rarity -

Scarcity

(edge configuration)

(setting for landforms or features-islands, outcrop

rocks, floating objects)

(contrast in texture)

Environment for Pleasing Life Forms

Vegetation - Riparian Associations - (Willows, cattails

Lilypads, fish amphibians, butterflies, others, etc.)

Geological sculpturing and weathering (cutting, smoothing,

polishing, staining)

Ice

Vapor-mist

Factors such as these could thus be systematically facilitated in design or management practice. It is not intended to suggest that the above is necessarily a complete - or even correct - list. An adequate catalog of water resource principles will emerge only as research findings accumulate.

There are several reasons for conducting empirical research rather than relying on common sense indications. First, common sense is occasionally wrong. Second, it often does not specify the precise conditions under which a given phenomenon (or aesthetic response) will occur. For example, while ice might ordinarily be considered to contribute to aesthetic experience, there are no doubt conditions under which it degrades aesthetic response. Finally, there are always aspects or situations for which common sense (or the planner-manager's intuition) has little or nothing to say.

2. Factors which generally detract from or decrease aesthetic satisfaction

Specification of the factors universally regarded as detri-mental to the aesthetic experience will serve as similarly useful data for professionals. These factors - situations, qualities, and/or attributes - would represent a set of things to be avoided in water resource planning and might

be employed by water resources personnel in a manner

similar to those listed above. Such a list might include

the following:

Factors that can generally be expected to <u>decrease</u> aesthetic

satisfaction:

Floatable man-introduced debris-garbage, paper, suds,
  oil

Increased turbidity - decrease of natural clarity. Silt.

Presence of unnatural colors

Drawdown of water level from usual or natural levels -
  exposure of bottom or shoreline sides

Decrease usual or natural flow to stagnant conditions -
  fish kills, smell, pests

Attraction of annoying pests - insects, snakes, rodents,
  trash fish   .

Algal blooms, proliferation of weed plants

Evidence of dead or sickly wildlife, or fish

Unpleasant smells

Activity eroding banks, vegetative debris across banks
  and into water body

Noise from human activity

Crowding of area users

Flood flows of a destructive or threatening magnitude

Vandalism, overuse and deterioration of facilities,
  vegetation, ground cover

Hazards and barriers

Again, this list is intended to be suggestive, and must
await further research.

3. <u>Factors which are a function of the observer</u>

Since aesthetic response (as described in the simplified
model in the introduction) involves an interaction of
observer (or user) and the environment, it is important
to identify those aesthetic factors on which people are
not in agreement, and to determine the psychological
correlates of significant response patterns. For example,
it is likely that conservationist groups will regard a
particular developed water resource differently than will
a group of water engineers.

Any water resource planning which claims to meet specific
user desires or needs ought to take into account the specific
environmental dispositions of the like users. A number of
different classes of personal variables seem useful for
describing and distinguishing among groups of people who
respond differently to the same water resource. They include:

a. <u>Demographic variables</u>: A number of studies have shown
that such variables as socio-economic status, age, sex,
and stage in the life cycle are useful descriptors
with interesting relationships to aesthetic response
(Sonnefeld, 1966, Lowenthal, 1967, Lucas, 1964). Much
more work is needed in this area, however.

b. <u>Environmental dispositions</u>: This term has been used recently to describe significant patterns of environmental attitudes, beliefs, and values (McKechne, 1970). Soon we may find strikingly different aesthetic preferences between "pastoral" and "urban" types of people. Data of this sort is usually "deeper" and psychologically richer than demographic data.

c. <u>Symbolic associations</u>: People differ in the symbolic associations they have to water (and water resources). These associations may provide a key to understanding people's aesthetic preferences. Some examples of symbolic associations for water are: purity, power, timelessness, refreshment, life support, wildness, distance, serenity, continuousness, challenging (to navigate or cross), unpredictability. This area is essentially unexplored.

d. <u>Behaviors</u>: Certainly <u>what</u> a person is doing in relation to the water resource will in part determine <u>how</u> he experiences it. Behaviors are often powerful variables for understanding aesthetic response. In analyzing the asethetic experience reported by a person, it is important for us to know whether he was fishing, swimming, boating, sailing, scuba diving, canoeing, water-skiing, rowing, meditating, photographing, wildlife

watching, collecting, or simply passing by. Knowledge of the associated behaviors or activities of
the observer allows us to make better inferences
about his mental set at the time of the experience
of interest. These activity variables may themselves
be arrayed on such descriptive dimensions as active
vs. passive, social vs. solitary, equipment-bound
(or related) vs. free from artifacts, etc.

BIBLIOGRAPHY

ABT Associates. 1969. Water and the Cities. Prepared by ABT
Associates for the Office of Water Resources Researc, Dept.
of Interior. 507 pp.

Aguar, Charles E. 1970. "Minnesota Ironing Out its Pitted Ore
Region." Landscape Architecture Quarterly, April 1970.

Alexander, Harold E. and Arkansas Committee on Stream Preservation.
1968. Stream Preservation in Arkansas. Arkansas Committee on
Stream Preservation and the Arkansas Planning Commission. 92 pp.

American Society of Planning Officials. 1959. "Waterfronts:
Planning for Resort and Residential Uses." American Society of
Planning Officials. August 1959. 40 pp.

Anthos. 1969. "Water and Gardens and Landscape" Anthos (Swiss
Federation of Landscape Architects) Number 3, pp. 1-25.

Appleyard, D., K. Lynch and Meyer, J. 1964. View from the Road.
MIT Press, Cambridge, Mass. 64pp.

Architecture Forum. 1960. "Waterfronts: Bright, Breathing Edges
of a City's Life." Architecture Forum, Vol. 112, pp. 140-145.

Progressive Architecture, 1966, "Back to the Waterfront:Chaos or
Control?" Progressive Architecture, V. 47(8).

"Back to the Waterfront:Chaos or Control?" Progressive Architecture,V. 47(8).

Bardach, John. 1964. Downstream: A Natural History of the River.
Harper and Row, New York. 278 pp.

Bauer, Anthony M. 1966. "How to Make More Than Holes in the
Ground." Landscape Architecture Quarterly, January 1966.

Beardsley, Monroe C. 1958. Aesthetics: Problems in the Philosophy
of Criticism. Harcourt Brace & Co., New York. 614 pp.

Boyle, Robert H. 1969. The Hudson River: A Natural and Unnatural
History. Norton Press, New York. 304 pp.

Brittain, Robert. 1958. Rivers, Man and Myths. Doubleday and Co.,
Garden City, N. Y. 288 pp.

Brower, David (ed.) 1964. Time and the River Flowing. Sierra
Club, San Francisco, Calif. 176 pp.

Burby, Raymond J. 1969. The Role of Reservoir Owner Policies in
Guiding Reservoir Land Development. North Carolina State
University, Water Resources Institute, Chapel Hill, N. C. 56 pp.

Burby, Raymond J. 1967. Lake Oriented Sub-divisions in North Carolina. University of North Carolina, Water Resources Research Institute, Chapel Hill, N. C. 177 pp.

Burggraf and King. 1967. Susquehanna River Basin: Natural Resources and the Future. Prepared for the National Park Service, Washington. 67 pp.

Cain, Stanley A. 1968. "Ecological Impacts on Water Resources Development." Water Resources Bulletin, Vol. 4, No. 1, 57-71. March 1968.

California Resources Agency. 1971. California Protected Waterways Plan. California Resources Agency, Protected Waterways Program, Sacramento, Calif. 111 pp.

California State Legislative Assembly Interim Committee on Natural Resources. 1967. Man's Effect on California Watersheds. California State Legislative Assembly Interim Committee on Natural Resources, Planning and Public Works, Sacramento.

Candeub, Fleissig, and Associates. 1968. Region Design Study: The Forms and Appearances of the Tampa Bay Region. Tampa Bay Regional Planning Council, St. Petersburg, Fla. 120 pp.

Clawson, Marion and Knetsch, Jack L. 1966. Economics of Outdoor Recreation. Baltimore: John Hopkins Press for Resources for the Future, Inc. 328 pp.

Coppedge, R. O. and J. R. Gray. 1967. Recreational Use and Value of Water on Elephant Butte and Navajo Reservoirs. New Mexico State University Agricultural Experiment Station, Bulletin 535. 24 pp.

Craighead, Frank and John Craighead. 1962. "River Systems-Recreational Classification, Inventory and Evaluation." Naturalist 13(2) 3-19. Summer 1962.

Craik, Kenneth H. 1970. "Environmental Psychology." New Directions in Psychology - IV. Hold, Rinehart and Winston, New York. 125 pp.

_____ 1968. "Human Responsiveness to Landscape: An Environmental Psychological Perspective." Student Publication of the School of Design, North Carolina State University, Raleigh, N. C.

Crowe, Sylvia and Browne, Kenneth. 1959. "Reservoirs." Architectural Review, Vol. 117, 331-335. May 1959.

Cullen, Gordon. 1953. "Immediacy." Architectural Review, Vol. 113, 235-239. April 1953.

Dasmann, Raymond F. 1968. A Different Kind of Country. Macmillan Co., New York. 276 pp.

David, Elizabeth L. 1968. "Lakeshore Property Values: Guide to Public Investment in Recreation." Water Resources Research 4(4) 697-707. August 1968.

David, Elizabeth L. and William B. Lord. 1969. "Determinants of Property Value on Artificial Lakes." (Unpublished report University of Wisconsin, College of Agriculture, Madison, Wisc.) 55 pp.

Davidson, Gladney G. 1970. Streams and Stream Preservation - Justification for a Scenic Rivers Program in Louisiana. Louisiana Wildlife and Fisheries Commission, Baton Rouge. 107 pp.

Dearinger, John A. 1968. Esthetic and Recreational Potential of Small Naturalistic Streams Near Urban Areas. University of Kentucky, Water Resources Institute, Lexington. 260 pp.

DeWolfe, Ivy. 1967. "Waterside Trim: Illustrated by Examples from Lake Geneva." Architectural Review, Vol. 141, 260-270. April 1967.

Ditton, Robert B. 1969. The Identification and Critical Analysis of Selected Literature Dealing with the Recreational Aspects of Water Resource Use, Planning and Development. University of Illinois, Water Resources Center, Urbana, Ill. 293 pp.

Elliot, Charles W. 1961. A Preliminary Planning Study of the Banks of the Charles River. Commonwealth of Massachusetts, Metropolitan District Commission, Cambridge. 46 pp.

George Washington University. 1962. Shoreline Recreation Resources of the United States. A report prepared for the U. S. Outdoor Recreation Resources Review Commission. 156 pp.

Gibberd, Frederick. 1967. "The Landscaping of Reservoirs." Architectural Review, Vol 141, 182-194. March 1967.

Gibson, James J. 1950. Perception of the Visual World. Houghton Mifflin Co., Boston.

Gilbert, J. B. 1968. "Aesthetics in the Design of Water Facilities." American Waterworks Association Journal, Vol. 60(2) 243-252.

Gill, J. C. 1969. "Lakeside Buildings and Marinas." Lancaster Conference (English) Institute of Landscape Architects Annual Conference, September 1969. 13 pp.

Gray, John. 1970. An Approach to Design and Planning for Outdoor Recreation: Two Case Studies in Water-Oriented Recreation Areas. (Unpublished M. A. thesis, University of California, College of Environmental Design, Berkeley.)

Hendee, J. C. 1969. "Appreciative versus Consumptive Uses of Wildlife Refuges: Studies of who gets what and trends in use." Transactions of the 34th North American Wildlife and Natural Resources Conference, March 1969. Wildlife Management Institute, Washington, D. C. p 252-264.

Hendee, J. C., W. R. Catton, L. D. Marlow and C. F. Brockman. 1968. Wilderness Users in the Pacific Northwest - Their Characteristics, Values, and Management Preferences. USDA, Forest Serv., Pacific Northwest Forest and Range Experiment Sta, Portland. 92 pp.

Herbst, John and Edgar Michalson. 1970. A Wild and Scenic Rivers Symposium. University of Idaho, Water Resources Research Institute, Information Bulletin No. 6. 40 pp.

Herfindahl, Orris C. and Allen V. Kneese. 1965. Quality of the Environment. Resources for the Future, Inc., Baltimore. 96 pp.

Hewston, John D. 1969. Recreational Use Pattern at Flaming Gorge Reservoir. USDI, Fish and Wildlife Service, Washington. 80 pp.

Hubbard, Henry V. and Theodora Kimball. 1917. An Introduction to the Study of Landscape Design. Macmillan Co., New York. 442 pp, illus.

Ingham, J. K. 1969. "Building by the Water's Edge." Lancaster Conference (English) Institute of Landscape Architects Annual Conference, September 1969. 4 pp.

Iowa State University, Department of Landscape Architecture. 1969. Souris-Red-Rainy River Basins: An Aesthetic Evaluation. A Report prepared for the National Park Service. 54 pp.

Jaackson, Reiner. 1970. "A Method to Analyze the Effects of Fluctuating Reservoir Water Levels on Shoreline Recreation Use." Water Resources Research, Vol. 6, No. 2, 421-429.

Johnson, Craig and Sand and Gravel Institute. 1966. "South Santa Fe Exercise." Reclamation of Mining Scars, Landscape Architecture Quarterly. Vol. 56, No. 2.

Kassler, Elizabeth B. 1959. "Water Inside and Out." <u>Architectural Record</u>, Vol. 125, 165-174. June 1959

_____ 1959. "Why Water?" <u>Architectural Record</u>, Vol. 125, 189-196. May 1959.

_____ 1958. "Water and Architecture." <u>Architectural Record</u>, Vol. 123, 137-152.

Kelnhofer, Guy J. 1968. <u>Metropolitan Planning and River Basin Planning: Some Interrelationships</u>. Georgia Institute of Technology, Altanta. 192 pp.

Kepes, Gyorgy. 1949. <u>Language of Vision</u>. P. Theobald, Chicago. 228 pp.

Kluckhohn, F. R. and F. L. Strodtbeck. 1961. <u>Variations in Value Orientation</u>. Row-Peterson and Co., Evanston, Ill.

Kneese, Allen V. 1967. "Economics and the Quality of the Environment." <u>Social Sciences and the Environment</u>. University of Colorado Press, Boulder. (Garnsey and Hibbs, eds.) p. 174-176.

Knetsch, J. C. 1964. "Influence of Reservoir Projects on Land Values." <u>Journal of Farm Economics</u>, Vol. 46, 231-243.

Koffka, Kurt. 1935. <u>Principles of Gestalt Psychology</u>. Harcourt-Brace, New York.

Krutilla, John. 1970. "Economic Analysis of Proposal to Develop the Snake River in Lower Hells Canyon." U. S. Senate Testimony, U. S. Government Printing Office, Washington, D. C. 57 pp.

Laurie, Ian C. 1965. <u>Tyne Landscape: A Survey of the River Corridor with Proposals for Landscape Renewal</u>. Consultants report to Newcastle upon Tyne, England. 2 volumes, unpaged.

Leopold, Luna B. 1969. "The Rapids and the Pools - Grand Canyon." <u>The Colorado River Region and John Wesley Powell</u>. U. S. Geological Survey Professional Paper 669. Washington, D.C., p. 131-145.

_____ 1969. "Quantitative Comparison of Some Aesthetic Factors Among Rivers." U. S. Geological <u>Survey Circulars</u> No. 620, Washington, D. C. 16 pp.

_____ 1968. "Hydrology for Urban Planning - A guidebook on the hydrologic effects of urban land use." U. S. Geological <u>Survey Circular</u> No. 554. Washington, D. C. 18 pp.

_____ 1962. "Rivers." <u>American Scientist</u>, Vol. 50, No. 4. p. 510 - 534.

304

Leopold, Luna B and M. O. Marchand. 1968. "On the Quantitative
Inventory of the Riverscape." Water Resources Research, Vol 4,
No. 4, 709-717.

Leopold L. B. and M. G. Wolman. 1957. "River Channel Patterns:
Braided, Meandering and Straight." U. S. Geological Survey
Professional Paper 282-B.

Leopold, L. B, M. G. Wolman and Miller J. P. 1964. Fluvial
Processes in Geomorphology. W. H. Freeman & Co., San Francisco
and London. 522 pp.

Lewis, P. H., Jr. 1968. Upper Mississippi River Comprehensive Basin
Study. (Appendix B: Aesthetic and Cultural Values). U.S.D.I,
National Park Service, Northeast Region, Kaukoma, Wisc. 312 pp.

_____ 1964. "Quality Corridors for Wisconsin." Landscape Architecture, vol. 54, No. 2, 100-108.

Licklider, Heath. 1965. Architectural Scale. George Braziller,
New York. 232 pp.

Litton, R. Burton, Jr. 1971. "Visual Landscape Units of the Lake
Tahoe Region." Scenic Analyses of the Lake Tahoe Region. U.S.D.A,
Forest Service, South Lake Tahoe, Calif. p. 6 - 14.

_____ 1968. Forest Landscape Description and
Inventories - a basis for land planning and design. U.S.D.A.,
Forest Service, Pacific Southwest Forest and Range Experiment Station
Res. Paper PSW-49, Berkeley, Calif. 64 pp., illus.

Litton, R. Burton, Jr. with Craik, K. H. 1970. Aesthetic Dimensions
of the Landscape. (Unpublished manuscript for Resources for the
Future, Inc., Washington, D. C.)

Lockwood, Donald. 1966. "Shoreline Problems in Reservoir Recreation
Areas." (Unpublished M.A. thesis, University of California, Department of Landscape Architecture., Berkeley.)

Lowenthal, David, (ed.) 1967. Environmental Perception and Behavior.
University of Chicago, Department of Geography, Research Paper,
Chicago, Ill. 88 pp.

Lucas, Robert. 1964. "User Concepts of Wilderness and their
Implications for Resource Management." Western Resource Papers.
University of Colorado, Boulder.

Lucas, Robert. 1964. Recreational Capacity of the Quetico-Superior Area. U.S.D.A., Forest Service, North Central Forest Experiment Station, Res. Paper LS-15, St. Paul, Minnesota.

_____ 1964. Recreational Use of the Quetico Superior Area. U.S.D.A., Forest Service, North Central Forest Experiment Station, Res. Paper LS-8, St. Paul, Minnesota.

Luckeish, M. 1922. Visual Illustrations and their Applications. D. Van Nostrand Co., New York.

McEvoy, James and Sharon Williams. 1970. Visual Pollution in the Lake Tahoe Basin. University of California, Tahoe Research Group, Davis, Calif. 24 pp.

McKechnie, G. E. 1970. "Measuring Environmental Dispositions with the Environmental Response Inventory." Proceedings of the Second Annual Environmental Design Research Association Conference, Philadelphia October 1970. 12 pp.

McQuade, Walter. 1961. "The Suffering Shoreline." Architecture Forum, Vol. 114, 90-97.

Maryland Department of State Planning, Scenic Rivers Review Board. 1970. Scenic Rivers in Maryland. Maryland Department of State Planning, Scenic Rivers Review Board, Annapolis. 40 pp.

Maryland, State of. The Governor's Patuxent River Watershed Advisory Committee. U. S. Federal Water Pollution Control Administration. 1968. The Patuxent River: Maryland's Asset, Maryland's Responsibility. Maryland State Planning Department, Annapolis. 50 pp.

Mason, Herbert L. 1970. The Scenic, Scientific and Educational Values of the Natural Landscape of California. State of California, Department of Parks and Recreation, Sacramento. 36pp.

Massachusetts, Commonwealth of, Metropolitan Area Planning Council, Metropolitan District Commission, Department of Natural Resources. 1969. Open Space and Recreation Program for Metropolitan Boston - Volume 3: The Mystic, Charles and Neponset Rivers. Commonwealth of Massachusetts, Boston. 71 pp.

Massachusetts, University of. 1967. Selected Resources of the Island of Nantucket (E. H. Zube, ed.) University of Massachusetts, Cooperative Extension Service, Amherst, Mass. 135 pp.

306

Massachusetts, University of. 1966. Springfield and the Connecticut River. University of Massachusetts, Cooperative Extension Service, Amherst, Mass. 97 pp.

Meier, R. L. 1969. "Resource Conserving Cities IV: The Differentiation of Life Styles." (Unpublished draft for the University of Michigan, Metal Health Research Institute, Ann Arbor, Mich.) 23 pp.

Michigan State University, Department of Resource Development. 1958. Shoretype Bulletins. Michigan State University, Department of Resource Development, Nos. 1-29., East Lansing, Mich.

Midwest Planning and Research, Inc. 1966. A Survey and Analysis of 24 Rivers in Minnesota. Midwest Planning and Research, Inc., St. Paul, Minn.

Milliken, J. G. and H. E. Mew. 1969. Economic and Social Importance of Recreation at Reclamation Reservoirs. University of Denver, Denver Research Institute, Denver, Colo. 145 pp.

Minnaert, M. 1954. The Nature of Light and Colour in the Open Air. Dover Publications, New York. 362 pp.

Moore, Charles W. "Water and Architecture." (Unpublished Ph.D. thesis, Princeton, University, 1957).

Morisawa, Marie. 1968. Streams: their Dynamics and Morphology. McGraw Hill Book Co., New York. 175 pp.

Morisawa, Marie and Martin Murie. 1969. Evaluation of Natural Rivers. Antioch College, Water Resources Research, Yellow Springs, Ohio. 143 pp.

Myles, George A. 1970. The Effect of Quality Factors on Water Based Recreation in Western Nevada. University of Nevada, Center for Water Resources Research, Reno. 62 pp.

_____ 1969. Participation in Water Based Recreation by Tourists. University of Nevada, Desert Research Institute, Reno.

Nash, Roderick (ed.) 1970. Grand Canyon of the Living Colorado. Ballantine Books and the Sierra Club, New York. 144 pp.

_____ 1967. Wilderness and the American Mind. Yale Univ. Press, New Haven, Conn. 256 pp.

National Parks and Conservation Association. 1963. "A Statement on the Basic Facts about Reservoir Drawdowns." National Parks and Conservation Association, Washington, D. C. 5 p.

Nighswonger, James J. 1970. A Methodology for Inventorying and Evaluating the Scenic Quality and Related Recreational Value of Kansas Streams. Kansas Department of Economic Development, Planning Division, Topeka, Kansas. 119 p.

Ohio Development Planning Institute. 1967. The Little Miami River of Ohio: A Study of a Wild and Scenic River. Athens, Ohio: Ohio Development Planning Institute. 56 pp.

Okamoto and Liskamm. 1967. Appearance and Design - Principles for Design and Development of San Francisco Bay. San Francisco Bay Conservation and Development Commission, San Francisco, Calif. 16 pp.

Pankey, Victor S. and W. E. Johnson. 1969. Analysis of Recreational Use of Selected Reservoirs in California. U. S. Dept. of Army Engineers, Washington, D. C. 42 pp.

Parr, A. E. 1967. "The Child in the City: Urbanity and the Urban Scene." Landscape, Vol. 16, 3-5.

Pepper, Stephen C. 1937. Aesthetic Quality. Charles Scribner's Sons, New York. 239 pp.

Peterson, George L. 1967. "A Model of Preference: Qualtitative Analysis of the Perception of Visual Appearance of Residential Neiborhoods." Journal of Regional Science, Vol. 7, No. 1, 19-31.

Peterson, George L. and Edward S. Neumann. 1969. "Modeling and Predicting Human Response to the Visual Recreation Environment." Journal of Leisure Research, Vol. 1, No. 3, 219-237.

Polakowski, Kenneth. 1970. Shoreland Planning in the Great Lakes Basin and Selected Coastal Zones of the United States. University of Michigan, Sea Grant Program, Ann Arbor, Mich. 126 pp.

Powell, John Wesley. 1961. The Exploration of the Colorado River. The Natural History Library, Anchor Books, Garden City, N. Y. 176 pp, illus.

Ragatz, Richard L. 1969. Vacation Homes. Cornell University, Dept. of Design and Environmental Analysis, Ithaca, N. Y. 387 pp.

Rapp, Charles Atlee. 1967. Water in the Urban Landscape: Fundamental Design Considerations. Unpub. masters thesis, Univ. of Calif. Berkeley. 94 pp.

Research, Planning and Design Associates. 1968. The Susquehanna
River Watershed: the Impact of Water on the Visual Landscape.
Research, Planning and Design Associates, Philadelphia. Prepared
for the U.S.D.I, National Park Service, Northeast Region. 38 pp.

_____ 1967. Study of the Visual and Cultural
Environment: North Atlantic Regional Water Resources Study.
North Atlantic Regional Water Resources Study Coordinating
Committee, Amherst, Mass. 71 pp.

Saarinen, T. F. 1969. "Perception of Environment." Association
of American Geographers, Commission on College Geography Resource
Paper Number 5. 27 pp.

_____ 1966. Perception of the Drought Hazard on the
Great Plains. University of Chicago, Department of Geography,
Research Paper No. 106, Chicago, Ill. 183 pp.

St. Croix Task Force. 1970. Wild Waters of the St. Croix.
St. Croix Task Force, Minneapolis, Minn. 78 pp.

Schumm, S. A. 1963. "Sinuosity of Alluvial Rivers on the Great
Plains." Bulletin of the Geologic Society of America, Vol. 2,
1089-1095.

Schutjer, W. A and M. C. Hallberg. 1968. "Impact of Water Recreational Development on Rural Property Values." American
Journal of Agricultural Economics, Vol. 50, 522-583.

Schutjer, W. A., R. Downing and M. C. Hallberg. 1968. "Recreational Water Reservoir Development and Rural Property Values."
Pennsylvania Argicultural Experiment Station Bulletins No. 749.

Scovel, J. L., E. J. O'Brian, J. C. McCormick, et al. 1965.
Atlas of Landforms. John Wiley & Sons, Inc., New York. 164 pp.,
illus

Shafer, Elwood L., John F. Hamilton and E. A. Schmidt. 1969.
"Natural Landscape Preferences: A predictive model." Journal
of Leisure Research, 1(1) 1-19.

Sierra Club. 1970. The Tuolumne River: A report on conflicting
goals with emphasis on the middle river. Tuolumne River Conference, Northern California Regional Conservation Committee,
Modesto, Calif. 80 pp.

Simonds, J. O. 1961. Landscape Architecture - the shaping of
man's natural environment. F. W. Dodge Corp., New York. 244 pp.,
illus

Smith, Winfield. 1969. Natural Waterways Study: An Element of the Santa Rosa Area General Plan. Santa Rosa Planning Dept., Santa Rosa, Calif. 68 pp.

Sonnenfeld, J. 1966. "Variable Values in Space and Landscape: An Inquiry into the Nature of Environmental Necessity." Journal of Social Issues, Vol. 22(4), 71-82.

Stanton, Boles, Maguire and Church. 1966. A Report on Appearance Planning. Bonneville Power Administration, Portland, Ore. 50 pp., illus.

Steinitz, Carl and Douglas Way. 1970. "A Model for Evaluating Visual Consequences of Urbanization on Shoreline Landscapes." A Study of Resource Use in Urbanized Watersheds. U. S. Army Corps of Engineers. 34 pp.

Parks & Recreation, 1966. "Storm over the Grand Canyon." Parks and Recreaction. June 1966, 496-501.

Stott, Charles C. 1967. Criteria for Evaluating the Quality of Water Based Recreational Facilities. University of North Carolina, Water Resources Research Institute, Raleigh, N. C. 88 pp.

Strodtbeck, Fred and Gilbert F. White. 1970. Attitudes toward Water: An Interdisciplinary Exploration. (Unpublished working draft, University of Chicago, Department of Geography, Social Psychology Laboratory, Chicago, Ill.) 344 pp.

Tahoe Regional Planning Agency. 1971. Proprosed Regional Plan - Lake Tahoe Region, California-Nevada. Tahoe Regional Planning Agency, South Lake Tahoe, Calif. 67 pp.

Tahoe Regional Planning and U. S. D. A., Forest Service. 1971. Scenic Analysis of the Lake Tahoe Region - A Guide to Planning. Tahoe Regional Planning Agency and U. S. D. A., Forest Service, South Lake Tahoe, Calif. 37 pp.

Tampa Bay Regional Planning Council. 1970. Regional Design Guide: A Handbook of Design Criteria and Regulatory Measures for Improved Development Appearances in the Tampa Bay Region. Tampa Bay Regional Planning Council, St. Petersburg, Fla. 100 pp.

Tennessee Department of Conservation, Division of Planning and Development. 1970. Tennessee's Scenic Rivers. Tennessee Department of Conservation, Division of Planning and Development. 17 pp.

Tennessee Valley Authority. 1938. The Scenic Resources of the Tennessee Valley: A Descriptive and Pictoral Inventory. Tennessee Valley Authority, Knoxville, Tenn. 222 pp.

Thiel, Philip. 1961. "A Sequence-experiment Notation for Architectural and Urban Space." Town Planning Review, Vol. 32, 33-52.

Thoreau, Henry D. 1963. The River: Selections from the Journal of Henry David Thoreau. Twayne Publishers, New York. 244 pp.

_____ 1937. "Walden," "A Week on the Concord and Merrimack Rivers," "Cape Cod," "The Allegash and East Branch." Walden and Other Writings. Modern Library, New York. 732 pp.

Tunnard, Christopher. 1939. "The Adventure of Water." Architectural Review, Vol. 86, 99-102.

U. S. Army Corps of Engineers, Chicago District. 1971. "Lakeshore Physiography and Use." Conference on Shoreline and Coastal Zone Management in the Great Lakes, University of Michigan Sea Grant Program, May 1971. 22 pp

U. S. Army Corps of Engineers, Office of the Chief of Engineers. 1970. "Environmental Considerations in Construction Contracts." U. S. Army Corps of Engineers Circular No. 1110-2-109. 29 pp.

U. S. Army Corps of Engineers, Department of Interior and Department of Agriculture. 1969. Big South Fork, Cumberland River: Inter-agency Report. Washington, D. C. 137 pp.

U. S. Bureau of Outdoor Recreation. 1970. Islands of America. U. S. Government Printing Office, Washington, D. C. 95 pp.

_____ 1970. The Potomac Estuary: A Study of the Recreation, Fish and Wildlife Potential. (Draft Copy.) Washington, D. C. 139 pp.

_____ 1968. The Middle Missouri: A Study of Outdoor Recreation Potential. U. S. Government Printing Office, Washington, D. C. 103 pp.

_____ 1968. New England Heritage: The Connecticut River National Recreation Area Study. U. S. Government Printing Office, Washington, D. C. 92 pp.

_____ 1966. Focus on the Hudson, Evaluation of Proposals and Alternatives. U. S. Department of Interior, Bureau of Outdoor Recreation, Washington, D. C. 51 pp.

U. S. Bureau of Outdoor Recreation, Mid Continent Region. 1969.
The Future of a River: Choices and Values. U. S. Bureau of
Outdoor Recreation, Denver, Colo. 27 pp.

U. S. Bureau of Outdoor Recreation, Northeast Region. 1970.
"An Environmental Quality Rating System. (Unpublished draft,
U. S. Bureau of Outdoor Recreation, Philadelphia.) 58 pp.

U. S. Bureau of Outdoor Recreation, Pacific Northwest Region. 1968.
"Recreation Aspects of Alternative Water Resource Developments of
the Lower Middle Snake River." Department of the Interior Resource
Study of the Middle Snake. 64 pp.

U. S. Bureau of Reclamation. 1969. "Environmental Quality - Preservation and Enhancement." Bureau of Reclamation, Manual of
General Instructions, Part 376-1, Series 350. 30 pp.

U. S. Congress, Committee on Government Operations. 1970. "The
Potomac Edison Company's High Voltage Transmission Line and its
Esthetic Impact on the Chesapeake and Ohio Canal National Monu-
ment. U. S. Congress, House Report 91-1083. U. S. Government
Printing Office, Washington, D. C. 50 pp.

U. S. Congress, House. Subcommittee on National Parks and
Recreation. (89th Congress) Indiana Dunes National Lakeshore,
Hearings on. October 2, 1965/April 26, 1966. Series No. 89-19.
U. S. Government Printing Office, Washington, D. C. 138 pp.

_____ Pictured Rocks National Lakeshore, Hearings
on. October 5, 1965. Series No. 89-21. U. S. Government Printing
Office, Washington, D. C. 82 pp.

_____ Sleeping Bear Dunes National Lakeshore, Hearings
on. October 4, 1965/June 20, 1966. Series No. 89-20. U. S.
Government Printing Office, Washington, D. C. 190 pp.

U. S. Congress. House. Committee on Interior and Insular Affairs.
Subcommittee on National Parks and Recreation. 1968. National
Scenic Rivers System. U. S. Government Printing Office, Washing-
ton, D. C. 547 pp.

U. S. Dept. of Agriculture and U. S. Dept. of Interior. 1970.
Environmental Criteria for Electric Transmission Systems. U. S.
Government Printing Office, Washington, D. C. 52 pp., illus.

312

U. S. Department of Agriculture, Forest Service. 1969. River
Plan for the Middle Fork of the Clearwater River. U. S. Govt.
Printing Office, Washington, D. C.

_____ 1969. River Plan for the Rogue River in
Oregon. U. S. Govt. Printing Office, Washington, D. C.

_____ 1969. River Plan for the Middle Fork of the
Salmon River. U. S. Govt. Printing Office, Washington, D. C.

U. S. Department of Agriculture, Forest Service, Northern Region.
1969. River Plan for Wild and Scenic Rivers. U.S.D.A., Forest
Service, Missoula, Montana.

U. S. Department of Agriculture, Forest Service, Wyoming Forest
Study Team. 1971. Forest Management in Wyoming - Timber Harvest
and the Environment. U.S.D.A., Forest Service, Washington, D. C.
80 pp.

U. S. Department of Interior. 1969. Master Plan for the Rogue
River Component of the National Wild and Scenic Rivers System.
U. S. Government Printing Office , Washington, D. C.

_____ 1967. The Creek and the City - Urban
Pressures on a Natural Stream, Rock Creek Park and Metropolitan
Washington. U. S. Government Printing Office, Washington, D. C.
52 pp.

_____ 1967. Surface Mining and our Environment.
U. S. Department of Interior, Washington, D. C. 124 pp.

U. S. Department of Interior and Department of Agriculture. 1970.
Guidelines for Evaluating Wild, Scenic, and Recreation River
Areas Proposed for Inclusion in the National Wild and Scenic
Rivers System under Section 2, Public Law 90-542. U. S. Government
Printing Office, Washington, D. C. 12 pp.

U. S. Department of Interior and the Federal Interdepartmental Task
Force on the Potomac. 1968. The Nation's River - (A Report on
the Potomac). U. S. Department of Interior and Federal Interdepartmental Task Force on the Potomac. 128 pp.

U. S. Federal Power Commission. 1965. Report on Criteria and
Standards for Outdoor Recreation Developments at Hydroelectric
Projects. U. S. Government Printing Office, Washington, D. C.
7 pp.

U. S. Federal Water Pollution Control Administration. 1968. Report
of the Committee on Water Quality Criteria. U. S. Government
Printing Office, Washington, D. C. 234 pp.

U. S. Geological Survey. 1962. Water for Recreation: Value and
Opportunities. Outdoor Recreation Resources Review Commission,
Washington, D. C. 73 pp.

U. S. National Park Service. 1968. Proposed Buffalo National
River. U. S. Government Printing Office, Washington, D. C. 24 pp.

U. S. Potomac Planning Task Force. 1967. The Potomac - A Report
on its Imperiled Future and Guide for Its Orderly Development.
U. S. Government Printing Office, Washington, D. C. 103 pp.

U. S. President's Council on Recreation and Natural Beauty. 1968.
Report of the Working Committee on Utilities. U. S. President's
Council on Recreation and Natural Beauty, Washington, D. C.

Vallentine, H. R. 1967. Water in the Service of Man. Penguin
Books, London. 215 pp.

Veatch, J. O. and C. R. Humphrys. 1966. Water and Water Use
Terminology. Thomas Publishing Co., Kaukauna, Wisconsin. 375 pp.

Virginia Commission of Outdoor Recreation. 1969. Virginia's Scenic
Rivers. Virginia Commission of Outdoor Recreation, Richmond. 22 pp.

Water Resources Engineers, Inc. 1970. Wild Rivers: Methods for
Evaluation. Water Resources Engineers, Inc. Prepared for the
Office of Water Resources Research. Walnut Creek, Calif. 106 pp.

Landscape Architecture, 1959. "Waterscape, America's Explosive Love
Affair with Water." Landscape Architecture, Vol. 49, 230-248.

Whalley, J. M. 1969. "Treatment of the Water's Edge.
Lancaster Conference(English) Institute of Landscape Architects
Annual Conference, September 1969. 5 pp.

Whitman, Ira L. 1968. Uses of Small Urban River Valleys. U. S.
Army Corps of Engineers, Washington, D. C. 309 pp.

Wildavsky, A. 1967. "Aesthetic Power or the Triumph of the
Sensitive Minority over the Vulgar Mass: A Political Analysis of
the New Economics." Daedalus, Fall 1967. pp. 1115-1128.

Willeke, Gene. 1968. "Effects of Water Pollution in San Francisco
Bay." A Program in Engineering Economic Planning, Report EEP-29,
Stanford University, Palo Alto. 153 pp.

Wisconsin Chapter - Soil Conservation Society of America. 1969. Water Use Principles and Guidelines for Planning and Management in Wisconsin, Soil Conservation Society, Madison, Wisc. 96 pp.

Wisconsin Department of Resource Development. Landscape Analysis: Lake Superior South Shore Area, Wisconsin Department of Resource Development, Madison, Wisc. 58 pp.

_____ 1964. Recreational Potential of the Lake Superior South Shore Area. Report 1: Landscape Analysis Lake Superior South Shore Area, Wisconsin Department of Resource Development, Madison, Wisc.

_____ 1966. Waterfront Renewal, Wisconsin Department of Resource Development, Madison, Wisc. 68 pp.

Zube, Ervin H. 1963. Taconite and the Landscape - Lake Superior South Shore Area, Wisconsin Department of Resource Development, Madison, Wisc. 34 pp.

Zube and Dega Associates. 1964. Wisconsin's Lake Superior Shoreline, Wisconsin Department of Resource Development, Madison, Wisc. 42 pp.

Addendum

(Following three citations were omitted from the original bibliography)

Eisley, Loren. 1959. The Immense Journey. Vintage Books, Random House, Inc., New York. 210 pp.

Greenough, Horatio. 1947. Form and Function. University of California Press, Berkeley, Los Angeles, California.

McHarg, Ian L. 1969. Design With Nature. The Natural History Press, Garden City, New York. 197 pp.